KRAFT
Velveeta

Crowd-Pleasing
Recipes

Contents

KRAFT Velveeta
Party-Time

A VARIETY OF HOT AND COLD DIPS TO

JUMP-START YOUR NEXT CELEBRATION

Dips

VELVEETA Ultimate Queso Dip

Prep: 5 min. ● Total: 10 min.

- 1 lb. (16 oz.) **VELVEETA** Pasteurized Prepared Cheese Product, cut into ½-inch cubes
- 1 can (10 oz.) RO*TEL® Diced Tomatoes & Green Chilies, undrained

MIX VELVEETA and tomatoes in microwaveable bowl.

MICROWAVE on HIGH 5 min. or until **VELVEETA** is completely melted, stirring after 3 min.

SERVE with tortilla chips or assorted cut-up vegetables.

Makes 3 cups or 24 servings, 2 Tbsp. each.

SIZE-WISE:

When eating appetizers at social occasions, preview your choices and decide which you'd like to try instead of taking some of each.

CREATIVE LEFTOVERS:

Cover and refrigerate any leftover dip. Reheat and serve over hot baked potatoes or cooked pasta.

SUBSTITUTE:

Prepare as directed, using VELVEETA Mild Mexican Pasteurized Prepared Cheese Product with Jalapeño Peppers.

*Ro*Tel® is a product of ConAgra Foods, Inc.*

Cheesy Spinach and Bacon Dip

Prep: 10 min. • Total: 10 min.

1 pkg. (10 oz.) frozen chopped spinach, thawed, drained

1 lb. (16 oz.) **VELVEETA** Pasteurized Prepared Cheese Product, cut into ½-inch cubes

4 oz. (½ of 8-oz. pkg.) **PHILADELPHIA** Cream Cheese, cut up

1 can (10 oz.) RO*TEL® Diced Tomatoes & Green Chilies, undrained

8 slices **OSCAR MAYER** Bacon, crisply cooked, drained and crumbled

COMBINE ingredients in microwaveable bowl.

MICROWAVE on HIGH 5 min. or until **VELVEETA** is completely melted and mixture is well blended, stirring after 3 min.

Makes 4 cups or 32 servings, 2 Tbsp. each.

VARIATION:

Prepare as directed, using VELVEETA Made With 2% Milk Reduced Fat Pasteurized Prepared Cheese Product and PHILADELPHIA Neufchâtel Cheese, ⅓ Less Fat than Cream Cheese.

HOW TO CUT UP VELVEETA:

Cut VELVEETA (the whole loaf) into ½-inch-thick slices. Then, cut each slice crosswise in both directions to make cubes.

CREATIVE LEFTOVERS:

Cover and refrigerate any leftover dip. Then, reheat and toss with your favorite hot, cooked pasta.

*Ro*Tel® is a product of ConAgra Foods, Inc.*

VELVEETA Chipotle Dip

Prep: 5 min. ● Total: 11 min.

1 lb. (16 oz.) **VELVEETA** Pasteurized Prepared Cheese Product, cut into ½-inch cubes

2 Tbsp. chipotle peppers in adobo sauce, chopped

1 container (16 oz.) **BREAKSTONE'S** or **KNUDSEN** Sour Cream

MIX VELVEETA and peppers in microwaveable bowl.

MICROWAVE on HIGH 4 to 6 min. or until **VELVEETA** is melted, stirring after 3 min. Stir in sour cream.

SERVE with assorted vegetable dippers.

Makes 3¼ cups or 26 servings, 2 Tbsp. each.

SIZE-WISE:

Savor every bite of this tasty, hot dip. Each 2-Tbsp. serving goes a long way on flavor.

TO HALVE:

Prepare as directed, cutting all ingredients in half. Makes about 1½ cups or 13 servings, about 2 Tbsp. each.

VELVEETA Chili Dip

Prep: 5 min. • Total: 10 min.

1 lb. (16 oz.) **VELVEETA** Pasteurized Prepared Cheese Product, cut into ½-inch cubes

1 can (15 oz.) chili with or without beans

MIX VELVEETA and chili in microwaveable bowl. Microwave on HIGH 5 min. or until **VELVEETA** is completely melted and mixture is well blended, stirring after 3 min.

SERVE hot with tortilla chips, **RITZ** Toasted Chips or assorted cut-up vegetables.

Makes 3 cups or 24 servings, 2 Tbsp. each.

HEALTHY LIVING:

Save 20 calories and 2 grams of fat per serving by preparing with VELVEETA Made With 2% Milk Reduced Fat Pasteurized Prepared Cheese Product.

HOW TO HALVE:

Mix ½ lb. (8 oz.) VELVEETA Pasteurized Prepared Cheese Product, cut up, and ¾ cup canned chili in 1-qt. microwaveable bowl. Microwave on HIGH 3 to 4 min. or until VELVEETA is melted, stirring after 2 min. Serve as directed. Makes 1¼ cups or 10 servings, 2 Tbsp. each.

TO SERVE A CROWD:

Mix 1½ lb. (24 oz.) VELVEETA Pasteurized Prepared Cheese Product, cut up, and 2 cups canned chili in 2½-qt microwaveable bowl on HIGH 4 min.; stir. Microwave 4 to 6 min. or until VELVEETA is melted, stirring every 2 min.; stir. Serve as directed. Makes 5 cups or 40 servings, 2 Tbsp. each.

VELVEETA Salsa Dip

Prep: 5 min. ● Total: 10 min.

1 lb. (16 oz.) **VELVEETA** Pasteurized Prepared Cheese Product, cut
  into ½-inch cubes

1 cup **TACO BELL® HOME ORIGINALS®** Thick 'N Chunky Salsa

COMBINE ingredients in microwaveable bowl. Microwave on HIGH
5 min. or until **VELVEETA** is completely melted and mixture is well
blended, stirring after 3 min.

SERVE hot with tortilla chips, assorted cut-up fresh vegetables or **RITZ**
Toasted Chips Original.

Makes 2½ cups or 20 servings, 2 Tbsp. each.

HEALTHY LIVING:

Save 20 calories and 2.5 g of fat per serving by preparing with VELVEETA
Made With 2% Milk Reduced Fat Pasteurized Prepared Cheese Product.

HOW TO CUT UP VELVEETA:

Cut VELVEETA (the whole loaf) into ½-inch-thick slices. Then, cut each slice
crosswise in both directions to make cubes.

VELVEETA MEXICAN SALSA DIP:

Prepare as directed, using VELVEETA Mild Mexican Pasteurized Prepared
Cheese Product with Jalapeño Peppers.

*TACO BELL® and HOME ORIGINALS® are trademarks owned and licensed by Taco
Bell Corp.*

VELVEETA Ranch Dip

Prep: 5 min. ● Total: 11 min.

1 lb. (16 oz.) **VELVEETA** Pasteurized Prepared Cheese Product, cut into ½-inch cubes

1 container (8 oz.) **BREAKSTONE'S** or **KNUDSEN** Sour Cream

1 cup **KRAFT** Ranch Dressing

MIX all ingredients in microwaveable bowl.

MICROWAVE on HIGH 6 min. or until **VELVEETA** is completely melted and mixture is well blended, stirring every 2 min.

SERVE with assorted cut-up vegetables or your favorite **NABISCO** Crackers.

Makes 3¼ cups or 26 servings, 2 Tbsp. each.

VELVEETA ZESTY RANCH DIP:

Add 1 can (10 oz.) undrained RO*TEL® Diced Tomatoes and Green Chilies to dip ingredients before microwaving. Increase the microwave time to 8 min., stirring every 2 min. Serve as directed.

VELVEETA PEPPER JACK RANCH DIP:

Prepare as directed, using VELVEETA Pepper Jack Pasteurized Prepared Cheese Product.

HOW TO SERVE IT COLD:

This versatile dip can also be served cold. Just prepare as directed; cool completely. Cover and refrigerate several hours or until chilled. Serve as directed.

*Ro*Tel® is a product of ConAgra Foods, Inc.*

VELVEETA Cheesy Bean Dip

Prep: 5 min. ● Total: 11 min.

1 lb. (16 oz.) **VELVEETA** Mild Mexican Pasteurized Prepared Cheese Product with Jalapeño Peppers, cut into ½-inch cubes

1 can (16 oz.) **TACO BELL® HOME ORIGINALS®** Refried Beans

½ cup **TACO BELL® HOME ORIGINALS®** Thick 'N Chunky Salsa

MIX all ingredients in microwaveable bowl.

MICROWAVE on HIGH 5 to 6 min. or until **VELVEETA** is completely melted and mixture is well blended, stirring after 3 min.

SERVE hot with tortilla chips or assorted cut-up vegetables.

Makes 3¼ cups or 26 servings, 2 Tbsp. each.

USE YOUR STOVE:

Mix all ingredients in medium saucepan. Cook on medium-low heat until VELVEETA is completely melted and mixture is well blended, stirring frequently. Serve as directed.

BEAN DIP OLÉ:

Prepare as directed, omitting the salsa, using VELVEETA Pasteurized Prepared Cheese Product and adding 1 undrained 4-oz. can chopped green chilies.

JAZZ IT UP:

To serve in a bread bowl, cut a lengthwise slice from the top of 1 (1-lb.) round bread loaf. Remove center of loaf, leaving 1-inch-thick shell. Cut loaf top and remove bread into bite-sized pieces to serve with dip. Fill bread bowl with hot dip just before serving.

TACO BELL® and HOME ORIGINALS® are trademarks owned and licensed by Taco Bell Corp.

Hot Broccoli Dip

Prep: 30 min. • Total: 30 min.

1 loaf (1½ lb.) round sourdough bread

½ cup chopped celery

½ cup chopped red bell peppers

¼ cup chopped onions

2 Tbsp. butter or margarine

1 lb. (16 oz.) **VELVEETA** Pasteurized Prepared Cheese Product, cut into ½-inch cubes

1 pkg. (10 oz.) frozen chopped broccoli, thawed, drained

¼ tsp. dried rosemary leaves, crushed

Few drops hot pepper sauce

PREHEAT oven to 350°F. Cut slice from top of bread loaf; remove center, leaving 1-inch-thick shell. Cut removed bread into bite-sized pieces. Cover shell with top of bread; place on baking sheet with bread pieces. Bake 15 min. Cool slightly.

MEANWHILE, cook and stir celery, red bell peppers and onions in butter in medium saucepan on medium heat until tender. Reduce heat to low. Add **VELVEETA**; cook until melted, stirring frequently. Add broccoli, rosemary and hot pepper sauce; mix well. Cook until heated through, stirring constantly.

SPOON into bread loaf. Serve hot with toasted bread pieces, **NABISCO** Crackers and/or assorted cut-up vegetables.

Makes 2½ cups or 20 servings, 2 Tbsp. each.

USE YOUR MICROWAVE:

Mix celery, red bell peppers, onions and butter in 2-qt. microwaveable bowl. Microwave on HIGH 1 min. Add VELVEETA, broccoli, rosemary and hot pepper sauce; mix well. Microwave 5 to 6 min. or until VELVEETA is melted, stirring after 3 min.

VARIATION:

Omit bread loaf. Spoon dip into serving bowl. Serve with crackers and assorted cut-up vegetables as directed.

Party-Time Dips 17

VELVEETA Southwestern Corn Dip

Prep: 5 min. ● Total: 10 min.

1 lb. (16 oz.) **VELVEETA** Pasteurized Prepared Cheese Product, cut into ½-inch cubes

1 can (11 oz.) corn with red and green bell peppers, drained

3 jalapeño peppers, seeded, minced

1 red onion, finely chopped

½ cup fresh cilantro, finely chopped

½ cup **BREAKSTONE'S** or **KNUDSEN** Sour Cream

MIX VELVEETA and corn in large microwaveable bowl. Microwave on HIGH 5 min. or until **VELVEETA** is completely melted, stirring after 3 min.

STIR in remaining ingredients.

SERVE hot with **WHEAT THINS** Snack Crackers or assorted cut-up fresh vegetables.

Makes 3½ cups or 28 servings, 2 Tbsp. each.

TO HALVE:

Mix ingredients as directed in 1-qt. microwaveable bowl, cutting all ingredients in half. Microwave on HIGH 3 to 4 min. or until VELVEETA is completely melted, stirring after 2 min. Serve as directed. Makes 1½ cups or 12 servings, 2 Tbsp. each.

KEEPING IT SAFE:

Hot dips should be discarded after setting at room temperature for 2 hours or longer.

HOW TO MAKE IT SPICY:

Save the seeds from one of the jalapeños and add to the dip. Or if you like it really fiery, no need to seed the peppers at all. Simply slice off the stems and chop.

VELVEETA Spicy Sausage Dip

Prep: 5 min. ● Total: 10 min.

1 lb. (16 oz.) **VELVEETA** Pasteurized Prepared Cheese Product, cut into ½-inch cubes

½ lb. pork sausage, cooked, drained

1 can (10 oz.) RO*TEL® Diced Tomatoes & Green Chilies, undrained

MICROWAVE all ingredients in large microwaveable bowl on HIGH 5 min. or until **VELVEETA** is completely melted, stirring after 3 min.

SERVE hot with tortilla chips or **WHEAT THINS** Snack Crackers.

Makes 1 qt. or 32 servings, 2 Tbsp. each.

STORAGE KNOW-HOW:

Store leftover dip in airtight container in refrigerator up to 3 days. Reheat dip in microwave before serving.

*Ro*Tel® is a product of ConAgra Foods, Inc.*

Cheesy Hawaiian Dip

Prep: 20 min. • Total: 20 min.

1 round loaf Hawaiian bread (1 lb.)

1 lb. (16 oz.) **VELVEETA** Pasteurized Prepared Cheese Product, cut into ½-inch cubes

1 can (10 oz.) RO*TEL® Diced Tomatoes & Green Chilies, undrained

⅓ cup chopped red onions

1 pkg. (8 oz.) **OSCAR MAYER** Smoked Ham, chopped

1 can (8 oz.) crushed pineapple, drained

PREHEAT oven to 350°F. Cut slice from top of bread loaf; remove center of loaf, leaving 1-inch-thick shell. Place on baking sheet. Cut removed bread into bite-size pieces. Place in single layer around bread shell on baking sheet. Bake 8 to 10 min. or until lightly toasted, stirring cubes after 5 min. Cool slightly.

MEANWHILE mix **VELVEETA**, tomatoes and onions in large microwave-able bowl. Microwave on HIGH 5 min. or until **VELVEETA** is completely melted, stirring after 3 min. Stir in ham and pineapple. Pour into bread shell.

SERVE with reserved bread pieces and assorted fresh vegetable dippers.

Makes 4½ cups or 36 servings, 2 Tbsp. each.

SUBSTITUTE:

Prepare as directed, using VELVEETA Made With 2% Milk Reduced Fat Pasteurized Prepared Cheese Product.

CREATIVE LEFTOVERS:

Cover and refrigerate any leftover dip. Reheat and use as a cheesy sauce for hot baked potatoes or steamed broccoli florets.

*Ro*Tel® is a product of ConAgra Foods, Inc.*

VELVEETA Spicy Cheeseburger Dip

Prep: 5 min. • Total: 10 min.

1 lb. (16 oz.) **VELVEETA** Pasteurized Prepared Cheese Product, cut into ½-inch cubes

1 can (10 oz.) RO*TEL® Diced Tomatoes & Green Chilies, undrained

1 cup **KRAFT** Shredded Low-Moisture Part-Skim Mozzarella Cheese

½ lb. ground beef, cooked, drained

½ cup sliced green onions

MIX all ingredients except onions in large microwaveable bowl.

MICROWAVE on HIGH 5 min. or until **VELVEETA** is completely melted, stirring after 3 min. Stir in onions.

SERVE with assorted cut-up fresh vegetables.

Makes 4½ cups or 36 servings, 2 Tbsp. each.

USE YOUR STOVE:

Mix all ingredients except onions in medium saucepan. Cook on medium heat 5 to 7 min. or until VELVEETA Pasteurized Prepared Cheese Product is completely melted, stirring frequently. Stir in onions. Serve as directed.

*Ro*Tel® is a product of ConAgra Foods, Inc.*

VELVEETA Spicy Buffalo Dip

Prep: 5 min. ● Total: 10 min.

1 lb. (16 oz.) **VELVEETA** Pasteurized Prepared Cheese Product, cut into ½-inch cubes

1 cup **BREAKSTONE'S** or **KNUDSEN** Sour Cream

¼ cup cayenne pepper sauce for Buffalo wings

¼ cup **KRAFT** Natural Blue Cheese Crumbles

2 green onions, sliced

COMBINE VELVEETA, sour cream and pepper sauce in large microwave-able bowl. Microwave on HIGH 5 min. or until **VELVEETA** is completely melted, stirring after 3 min.

STIR in remaining ingredients.

SERVE hot with celery and carrot sticks.

Makes 2¾ cups or 22 servings, 2 Tbsp. each.

VARIATION:

Prepare as directed, using VELVEETA Made With 2% Milk Reduced Fat Pasteurized Prepared Cheese Product and BREAKSTONE'S Reduced Fat or KNUDSEN Light Sour Cream.

SERVE IT COLD:

This dip is also great served cold. Prepare as directed; cool. Cover and refrigerate several hours or until chilled. Serve as directed.

KEEPING IT SAFE:

Hot dips should be discarded after setting at room temperature for 2 hours or longer.

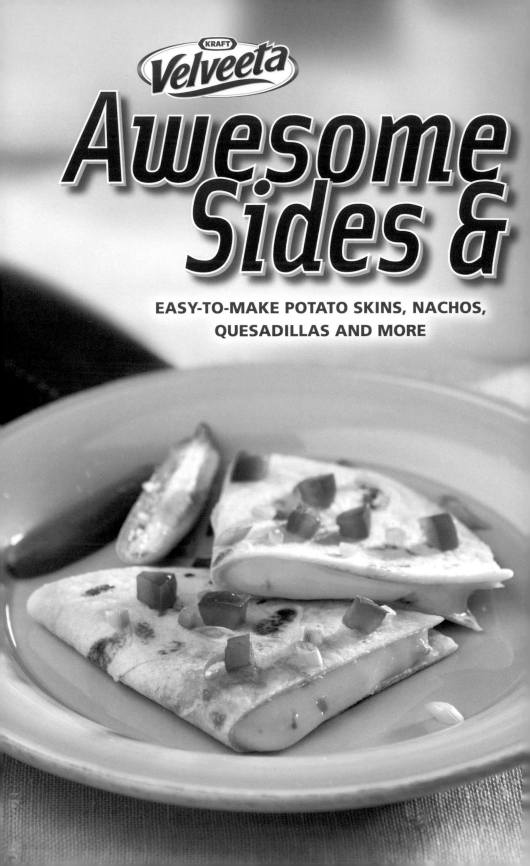

Appetizers, Snacks

Speedy Spicy Quesadillas

Prep: 5 min. • Total: 8 min.

½ lb. (8 oz.) Mild **VELVEETA** Mexican Pasteurized
Prepared Cheese Product with Jalapeño Peppers, cut
into 8 slices

8 flour tortillas (6 inch)

PLACE 1 **VELVEETA** slice on each tortilla. Fold tortillas in
half. Place 2 tortillas on microwaveable plate.

MICROWAVE on HIGH 30 to 45 sec. or until **VELVEETA** is
melted. Repeat with remaining tortillas.

CUT each quesadilla in half. Serve immediately.

Makes 8 servings, 2 quesadilla halves each.

SUBSTITUTE:

Prepare as directed, using VELVEETA Made With 2% Milk Reduced
Fat Pasteurized Prepared Cheese Product.

FOOD FACTS:

Flour tortillas, often used as soft taco shells, come in many colors
and sizes. Look for them in the dairy case or grocery aisle of the
supermarket. You'll also find them seasoned with herbs,
tomatoes, spinach or sesame seeds.

JAZZ IT UP:

Garnish with chopped fresh tomatoes and green onions.

Chicken Enchiladas

Prep: 20 min. ● Total: 40 min.

2 cups chopped cooked chicken or turkey

1 green bell pepper, chopped

4 oz. (½ of 8-oz. pkg.) **PHILADELPHIA** Cream Cheese, cubed

½ cup **TACO BELL® HOME ORIGINALS®** Thick 'N Chunky Salsa, divided

8 **TACO BELL® HOME ORIGINALS®** Flour Tortillas

¼ lb. (4 oz.) **VELVEETA** Pasteurized Prepared Cheese Product, cut into ½-inch cubes

1 Tbsp. milk

PREHEAT oven to 350°F. Mix chicken, green bell pepper, cream cheese and ¼ cup of the salsa in saucepan; cook on low heat until cream cheese is melted, stirring occasionally.

SPOON ⅓ cup of the chicken mixture down center of each tortilla; roll up. Place, seam-sides down, in lightly greased 13×9-inch baking dish. Place **VELVEETA** in small saucepan. Add milk; cook on low heat until **VELVEETA** is completely melted, stirring frequently. Pour over enchiladas; cover with foil.

BAKE 20 min. or until heated through. Top with remaining ¼ cup salsa.

Makes 4 servings, 2 enchiladas each.

SUBSTITUTE:

Prepare as directed, using PHILADELPHIA Neufchâtel Cheese, ⅓ Less Fat than Cream Cheese and VELVEETA Made With 2% Milk Reduced Fat Pasteurized Prepared Cheese Product.

SHORTCUT:

Substitute 1 pkg. (6 oz.) OSCAR MAYER Oven Roasted Chicken Breast Cuts for the chopped cooked fresh chicken.

TACO BELL® and HOME ORIGINALS® are trademarks owned and licensed by Taco Bell Corp.

Ultimate VELVEETA Nachos

Prep: 10 min. ● Total: 10 min.

1 lb. extra-lean ground beef

7 cups (6 oz.) tortilla chips

½ lb. (8 oz.) **VELVEETA** Pasteurized Prepared Cheese Product, cut into ½-inch cubes

1 cup shredded lettuce

½ cup chopped tomatoes

¼ cup sliced black olives

⅓ cup **BREAKSTONE'S** or **KNUDSEN** Sour Cream

BROWN meat; drain.

ARRANGE chips on microwaveable platter; top evenly with **VELVEETA**. Microwave on HIGH 2 min. or until **VELVEETA** is melted.

TOP with meat and remaining ingredients.

Makes 6 servings.

HEALTHY LIVING:

By preparing this dish with extra-lean ground beef (95% fat) instead of ground beef (80% fat), you will save 5g fat and 40 calories per serving.

JAZZ IT UP:

Season the meat with taco seasoning before spooning over the chips. Just brown the meat as directed. Then, add 1 pkg. (1¼ oz.) TACO BELL® HOME ORIGINALS® Taco Seasoning Mix and prepare as directed on package.

TACO BELL® and HOME ORIGINALS® are trademarks owned and licensed by Taco Bell Corp.

Cheesy Potato Skins

Prep: 15 min. ● Total: 35 min.

- 4 large baked potatoes
- 2 Tbsp. butter or margarine, melted
- ¼ lb. (4 oz.) **VELVEETA** Pasteurized Prepared Cheese Product, cut into ½-inch cubes
- 2 Tbsp. chopped red bell peppers
- 2 slices **OSCAR MAYER** Bacon, crisply cooked, crumbled
- 1 Tbsp. sliced green onions

PREHEAT oven to 450°F. Cut potatoes in half lengthwise; scoop out centers, leaving ¼-inch-thick shells. (Refrigerate removed potato centers for another use.) Cut shells crosswise in half. Place, skin-sides down, on baking sheet; brush with butter.

BAKE 20 to 25 min. or until crisp and golden brown.

FILL shells evenly with **VELVEETA**; continue baking until **VELVEETA** begins to melt. Top with remaining ingredients.

Makes 16 servings, 1 appetizer each.

SUBSTITUTE:

Substitute green bell peppers for the red bell peppers.

HOW TO BAKE POTATOES:

Russet potatoes are the best for baking. Scrub potatoes well, blot dry and rub the skin with a little oil and salt. Prick the skin of the potatoes with a fork so steam can escape. Stand them on end in a muffin tin. Bake at 425°F for 45 min. to 1 hour or until tender.

HOW TO USE GREEN ONIONS:

Green onions add a deliciously mild onion flavor to foods. To use them, trim off the roots and remove any wilted, brown or damaged tops, then slice and use as much of the white end and green shoot as you like.

VELVEETA Double-Decker Nachos

Prep: 15 min. • Total: 15 min.

6 oz. tortilla chips (about 7 cups)

1 can (15 oz.) chili with beans

½ lb. (8 oz.) **VELVEETA** Pasteurized Prepared Cheese Product, cut into ½-inch cubes

1 medium tomato, finely chopped

¼ cup sliced green onions

⅓ cup **BREAKSTONE'S** or **KNUDSEN** Sour Cream

ARRANGE half of the chips on large microwaveable platter; top with layers of half *each* of the chili and **VELVEETA**. Repeat layers.

MICROWAVE on HIGH 3 to 5 min. or until **VELVEETA** is melted.

TOP with remaining ingredients.

Makes 6 servings.

SIZE-WISE:
Enjoy your favorite foods while keeping portion size in mind.

SUBSTITUTE:
Prepare as directed, using VELVEETA Mild Mexican Pasteurized Prepared Cheese Product with Jalapeño Peppers.

Awesome Appetizers, Sides & Snacks

Fresh Vegetable Medley

Prep: 10 min. ● Total: 25 min.

1 small onion, chopped

1 Tbsp. margarine

½ lb. (8 oz.) **VELVEETA** Pasteurized Prepared Cheese Product, cut
   into ½-inch cubes

1 can (10¾ oz.) condensed cream of mushroom soup

8 cups mixed fresh vegetables (broccoli and cauliflower florets;
   sliced carrots, squash and zucchini; cut-up green beans; corn)

COOK and stir onions in margarine in large skillet on medium heat until
crisp-tender.

ADD VELVEETA and soup; cook until **VELVEETA** is completely melted
and mixture is well blended, stirring frequently.

STIR in remaining vegetables; cook 10 min. or until crisp-tender, stirring
frequently.

Makes 12 servings, 1½ cup each.

SHORTCUT:

**To shave even more time off this easy recipe, purchase cut-up fresh vegetables
from the supermarket salad bar. Or, substitute 2 pkg. (16 oz. each) frozen mixed
vegetables for the 8 cups mixed fresh vegetables.**

Awesome Appetizers, Sides & Snacks

Crispy Tostadas

Prep: 10 min. ● Total: 17 min.

8 tostada shells (5 inch)

1 can (16 oz.) **TACO BELL® HOME ORIGINALS®** Refried Beans

1 cup finely chopped red and green bell peppers

½ lb. (8 oz.) **VELVEETA** Pepper Jack Pasteurized Prepared Cheese Product, sliced

1 cup shredded lettuce

½ cup **TACO BELL® HOME ORIGINALS®** Thick 'N Chunky Salsa

PREHEAT oven to 350°F. Spread tostada shells with beans; top evenly with bell peppers and **VELVEETA**.

BAKE 5 to 7 min. or until **VELVEETA** is melted.

TOP with lettuce and salsa.

Makes 8 servings, 1 tostada each.

VARIATION-CRISPY BEEF TOSTADAS:

Omit refried beans. Brown 1 lb. lean ground beef in medium skillet; drain. Return to skillet. Add 1 pkg. (1¼ oz.) TACO BELL® HOME ORIGINALS® Taco Seasoning Mix; prepare as directed on package. Spoon meat mixture evenly onto tostada shells. Top with peppers and VELVEETA. Continue as directed.

SERVING SUGGESTION:

Serve with a tossed green salad drizzled with KRAFT Light Ranch Reduced Fat Dressing.

TACO BELL® and HOME ORIGINALS® are trademarks owned and licensed by Taco Bell Corp.

Cheesy Scramblin' Pizza

Prep: 10 min. ● Bake: 10 min.

 6 eggs

 ¼ cup milk

 ¼ cup sliced green onions

 1 small tomato, chopped

 1 Italian pizza crust (12 inch)

 ½ lb. (8 oz.) **VELVEETA** Pasteurized Prepared Cheese Product, cut
    into ½-inch cubes

 6 slices **OSCAR MAYER** Ready to Serve Bacon, cut into 1-inch pieces

PREHEAT oven to 450°F. Beat eggs, milk, onions and tomatoes with
wire whisk until well blended. Pour into medium skillet sprayed with
nonstick cooking spray. Cook on medium-low heat until eggs are set,
stirring occasionally.

PLACE pizza crust on baking sheet; top with egg mixture and
VELVEETA. Sprinkle with bacon.

BAKE 10 min. or until **VELVEETA** is melted. Cut into wedges to serve.

Makes 8 servings, 1 wedge each.

SERVING SUGGESTION:

For a delightful brunch idea, serve this Cheesy Scramblin' Pizza with a seasonal
fresh fruit salad.

VARIATION:

Prepare as directed substituting 6 English muffins, split, toasted, for the pizza
crust. Makes 12 servings.

SUBSTITUTE:
Substitute ½ lb. (8 oz.) VELVEETA Mild Mexican Pasteurized Prepared Cheese Product with Jalapeño Peppers for the VELVEETA Pasteurized Prepared Cheese Product.

Awesome Appetizers, Sides & Snacks

VELVEETA Cheesy Tortilla Corn

Prep: 10 min. • Total: 25 min.

4 green onions, sliced

½ cup chopped red peppers

1 Tbsp. margarine

2 pkg. (10 oz. each) frozen corn, thawed, drained

6 oz. **VELVEETA** 2% Milk Pasteurized Prepared Cheese Product, cut into ½-inch cubes

⅔ cup crushed tortilla chips

2 Tbsp. chopped fresh cilantro

COOK and stir onions and peppers in margarine in large skillet on medium-high heat until crisp-tender.

STIR in corn and **VELVEETA**; cook on medium-low heat 5 to 7 min. or until **VELVEETA** is completely melted and mixture is heated through, stirring occasionally.

SPOON into serving bowl; top with remaining ingredients.

Makes 6 servings

USE YOUR MICROWAVE:

Microwave onions, red peppers and margarine in 1½-qt. microwaveable bowl on HIGH 2 to 3 min. or until vegetables are tender. Stir in corn and VELVEETA. Microwave 5 to 7 min. or until VELVEETA is completely melted and mixture is heated through, stirring after 4 min.; mix well. Spoon into serving bowl and continue as directed.

5-Minute Cheesy Broccoli Toss

Prep: 5 min. • Total: 10 min.

4 cups frozen broccoli florets

½ tsp. dry mustard

¼ lb. (4 oz.) **VELVEETA** Pasteurized Prepared Cheese Product, cut into ½-inch cubes

1 Tbsp. **KRAFT** Grated Parmesan Cheese

COMBINE broccoli, mustard and **VELVEETA** in large nonstick skillet on medium-high heat.

COOK 5 min. or until broccoli is crisp-tender and mixture is heated through, stirring occasionally.

SPRINKLE with Parmesan.

Makes 4 servings, about ¾ cup each.

SPECIAL EXTRA:

Add 1 minced garlic clove with the broccoli.

Crowd-Plea Entrées

HEARTY DISHES FOR ANY GET-TOGETHER

Chicken Fiesta Chili Mac

Prep: 15 min. ● Total: 35 min.

1½ cups elbow macaroni, uncooked

1 lb. boneless, skinless chicken breasts, cut into strips

1 can (15 oz.) chili with beans

½ cup chopped green bell peppers

2 cloves garlic, minced

½ lb. (8 oz.) **VELVEETA** Pasteurized Prepared Cheese Product, cut into ½-inch cubes

½ cup **TACO BELL® HOME ORIGINALS®** Thick 'N Chunky Salsa

PREHEAT oven to 350°F. Cook macaroni as directed on package. Meanwhile, cook chicken in large nonstick skillet sprayed with cooking spray 5 to 7 min. or until cooked through, stirring frequently.

DRAIN macaroni. Add to chicken in skillet. Stir in chili, peppers, garlic, **VELVEETA** and salsa. Spoon into 13×9-inch baking dish sprayed with nonstick cooking spray.

BAKE 20 min. or until heated through. Stir before serving.

Makes 6 servings.

JAZZ IT UP:

For added heat, add 1 tsp. hot pepper sauce to the chicken mixture before spooning into prepared baking dish.

SERVING SUGGESTION:

Serve this family-pleasing main dish with a crisp tossed green salad.

TACO BELL® and HOME ORIGINALS® are trademarks owned and licensed by Taco Bell Corp.

Macaroni and Cheese Dijon

Prep: 20 min. ● Total: 45 min.

1¼ cups milk

½ lb. (8 oz.) **VELVEETA** Pasteurized Prepared Cheese Product, cut into ½-inch cubes

2 Tbsp. **GREY POUPON** Dijon Mustard

6 slices **OSCAR MAYER** Bacon, cooked, drained and crumbled

⅓ cup green onion slices

⅛ tsp. ground red pepper (cayenne)

3½ cups tri-colored rotini pasta, cooked, drained

½ cup French fried onion rings

PREHEAT oven to 350°F. Mix milk, **VELVEETA** and mustard in medium saucepan; cook on low heat until **VELVEETA** is completely melted and mixture is well blended, stirring occasionally. Add bacon, green onions and pepper; mix lightly. Remove from heat. Add to pasta in large bowl; toss to coat.

SPOON into greased 2-qt. casserole dish; cover.

BAKE 15 to 20 min. or until heated through. Uncover; stir. Top with onion rings. Bake, uncovered, an additional 5 min. Let stand 10 min. before serving.

Makes 6 servings, 1 cup each.

MAKE IT EASY:

For easy crumbled bacon, use kitchen scissors to snip raw bacon into ½-inch pieces. Let pieces fall right into skillet, then cook until crisp and drain on paper towels.

VELVEETA Chicken Enchilada Casserole

Prep: 15 min. • Total: 50 min.

- ¾ cup **TACO BELL® HOME ORIGINALS®** Thick 'N Chunky Salsa, divided
- 2 cups chopped cooked chicken
- 1 can (10¾ oz.) condensed cream of chicken soup
- ½ lb. (8 oz.) **VELVEETA** Mild Mexican Pasteurized Prepared Cheese Product with Jalapeño Peppers, cut into ½-inch cubes
- 6 corn tortillas (6 inch), cut in half

PREHEAT oven to 350°F. Reserve ¼ cup of the salsa for later use. Mix chicken, soup and **VELVEETA** until well blended. Spread 1 cup of the chicken mixture onto bottom of 8-inch square baking dish.

TOP with layers of 6 tortilla halves, ¼ cup of the remaining salsa and half of the remaining chicken mixture; repeat layers.

BAKE 30 to 35 min. or until heated through. Serve topped with the reserved ¼ cup salsa.

Makes 6 servings.

USE YOUR MICROWAVE:

Assemble as directed in 8-inch square microwaveable dish. Microwave on HIGH 10 to 14 min. or until heated through.

SERVING SUGGESTION:

Serve with bagged salad greens topped with your favorite KRAFT Dressing, such as Ranch.

TACO BELL® and HOME ORIGINALS® are trademarks owned and licensed by Taco Bell Corp.

VELVEETA Baked Spaghetti Squares

Prep: 15 min. ● Total: 50 min.

- 4 eggs
- ¼ cup milk
- 1 pkg. (16 oz.) spaghetti, cooked, drained
- 1 green bell pepper, chopped
- 1 can (7 oz.) mushroom pieces and stems, drained
- 1 small onion, chopped
- ½ lb. (8 oz.) **VELVEETA** Pasteurized Prepared Cheese Product, cut into ½-inch cubes
- ½ cup **KRAFT** 100% Grated Parmesan Cheese
- 1 jar (26 oz.) spaghetti sauce, warmed

PREHEAT oven to 350°F. Beat eggs and milk in large bowl with wire whisk until well blended. Add spaghetti, peppers, mushrooms, onions, **VELVEETA** and Parmesan cheese.

SPOON into 13×9-inch baking dish sprayed with cooking spray; press into dish with back of spoon.

BAKE 30 to 35 min. or until heated through. Cut into 8 squares. Serve each square topped with about ¼ cup of the spaghetti sauce.

Makes 8 servings.

VARIATION:

Prepare as directed, using VELVEETA Made with 2% Milk Reduced Fat Pasteurized Prepared Cheese Product and substituting 1 cup cholesterol-free egg product for the 4 eggs.

Cheesy Chicken & Broccoli Bake

Prep: 10 min. • Total: 40 min.

1 pkg. (6 oz.) **STOVE TOP** Stuffing Mix for Chicken

1½ lb. boneless, skinless chicken breasts, cut into 1-inch pieces

1 pkg. (16 oz.) frozen broccoli florets, thawed, drained

1 can (10¾ oz.) reduced-sodium condensed cream of chicken soup

½ lb. (8 oz.) **VELVEETA** Pasteurized Prepared Cheese Product, cut into ½-inch cubes

PREHEAT oven to 400°F. Prepare stuffing mix as directed on package.

MEANWHILE, combine remaining ingredients in 13×9-inch baking dish. Top with stuffing.

BAKE 30 min. or until chicken is cooked through.

Makes 6 servings.

SUBSTITUTE:

Substitute ¾ cup CHEEZ WHIZ Cheese Dip for the cubed VELVEETA.

VARIATION:

Prepare as directed, using VELVEETA Made With 2% Milk Reduced Fat Pasteurized Cheese Product.

VELVEETA Italian Sausage Bake

Prep: 25 min. • Total: 45 min.

1½ cups small penne pasta, uncooked

1 lb. Italian sausage, casings removed

4 small zucchini, halved lengthwise, sliced

1 red or green bell pepper, chopped

1 can (8 oz.) pizza sauce

½ lb. (8 oz.) **VELVEETA** Pasteurized Prepared Cheese Product, cut into ½-inch cubes

1½ cups **KRAFT** 100% Grated Parmesan Cheese

PREHEAT oven to 350°F. Cook pasta as directed on package. Meanwhile, brown sausage in large deep skillet on medium-high heat, stirring occasionally to break up the sausage. Drain; return sausage to skillet. Add zucchini, peppers and pizza sauce; stir until well blended. Cook 5 to 6 min. or until vegetables are tender, stirring occasionally. Drain pasta. Add to sausage mixture along with the **VELVEETA**; stir until well blended.

SPOON into 13×9-inch baking dish sprayed with nonstick cooking spray; sprinkle with Parmesan cheese.

BAKE 15 to 20 min. or until heated through.

Makes 6 servings.

KID FRIENDLY:

Prepare as directed, substituting 1 lb. lean ground beef for the sausage and 1 cup *each* shredded carrots and zucchini for the 3 cups sliced zucchini. Also, try using a fun pasta shape, such as wagon wheels.

VARIATION-VELVEETA SAUSAGE AND RICE CASSEROLE:

Omit pasta. Prepare as directed, adding 1½ cups uncooked instant white rice and 1½ cups water to the meat mixture along with the VELVEETA. Increase the baking time to 35 to 40 min. or until rice is tender and casserole is heated through. Makes 8 servings.

VELVEETA Ultimate Macaroni & Cheese

Prep: 20 min. ● Total: 20 min.

2 cups (8 oz.) elbow macaroni, uncooked

¾ lb. (12 oz.) **VELVEETA** Pasteurized Prepared Cheese Product, cut into ½-inch cubes

⅓ cup milk

⅛ tsp. black pepper

COOK macaroni as directed on package; drain well. Return to pan.

ADD remaining ingredients; mix well. Cook on low heat until **VELVEETA** is completely melted and mixture is well blended, stirring frequently.

Makes 4 servings, 1 cup each.

HEALTHY LIVING:

Save 70 calories and 10 grams of fat per serving by preparing with VELVEETA Made With 2% Milk Reduced Fat Pasteurized Prepared Cheese Product.

VARIATION:

Prepare as directed. Pour into 2-qt. casserole dish. Bake at 350°F for 25 min.

DRESSED-UP MAC 'N CHEESE:

Substitute bow-tie pasta or your favorite shaped pasta for the macaroni.

VELVEETA BBQ Bacon Cheeseburger Mac

Prep: 10 min. ● Total: 25 min.

1½ lb. ground beef

1 small onion, chopped

½ cup **BULL'S-EYE** or **KRAFT** Original Barbecue Sauce

2¾ cups water

2 cups (8 oz.) elbow macaroni, uncooked

½ lb. (8 oz.) **VELVEETA** Pasteurized Prepared Cheese Product, cut into ½-inch cubes

1 large tomato, chopped

½ cup **OSCAR MAYER** Real Bacon Recipe Pieces

BROWN meat with onion in large skillet on medium heat; drain. Add barbecue sauce and water; mix well. Bring to boil. Add macaroni; cook 8 to 10 min. or until macaroni is tender, stirring occasionally.

STIR in **VELVEETA**; cook until **VELVEETA** is completely melted and mixture is well blended, stirring occasionally.

TOP with the tomatoes and bacon pieces.

Makes 6 servings.

SERVING SUGGESTION:

Serve with a crisp green vegetable, such as steamed broccoli.

STORAGE KNOW-HOW:

Store ground meats in coldest part of refrigerator for up to 2 days. Make sure raw juices do not touch other foods. Ground meat can be wrapped airtight and frozen for up to 3 months.

SUBSTITUTE:

Substitute rotini for the elbow macaroni.

VELVEETA Easy Beef Taco Salad

Prep: 10 min. • Total: 30 min.

1 lb. ground beef

1 small onion, chopped

1 pkg. (1¼ oz.) **TACO BELL® HOME ORIGINALS®** Taco Seasoning Mix

¾ cup water

1 pkg. (10 oz.) frozen corn

½ lb. (8 oz.) **VELVEETA** Pasteurized Prepared Cheese Product, cut into ½-inch cubes

1 bag (8 oz.) shredded iceberg lettuce (about 4½ cups)

1 large tomato, chopped

6 oz. tortilla chips (about 9 cups)

BROWN meat with onions in large skillet on medium-high heat; drain. Add seasoning mix and water; cook as directed on package.

STIR in corn and **VELVEETA**; cover. Cook on low heat 5 min. or until **VELVEETA** is completely melted and mixture is well blended, stirring frequently.

SPOON over lettuce just before serving; top with tomatoes. Serve with tortilla chips.

Makes 6 servings, 1 cup each.

SIZE-WISE:

Let your kids help assemble these main-dish salads. As a bonus, they'll also learn about portion sizes.

SUBSTITUTE:

Substitute thawed frozen LOUIS RICH Pure Ground Turkey for the ground beef.

TACO BELL® and HOME ORIGINALS® are trademarks owned and licensed by Taco Bell Corp.

VELVEETA Tex-Mex Beef and Potatoes

Prep: 10 min. ● Total: 30 min.

1   lb. ground beef

1   red or green bell pepper, chopped

1   onion, chopped

1   pkg. (1¼ oz.) **TACO BELL® HOME ORIGINALS®** Taco Seasoning
    Mix

½   cup water

4   cups frozen Southern-style hash browns (cubed not shredded
    variety)

1   pkg. (10 oz.) frozen corn

½   lb. (8 oz.) **VELVEETA** Pasteurized Prepared Cheese Product, cut
    into ½-inch cubes

PREHEAT oven to 350°F. Brown meat with peppers and onions in large skillet on medium-high heat, stirring occasionally to break up the meat; drain. Return meat mixture to skillet.

ADD taco seasoning mix and water; stir until well blended. Stir in potatoes, corn and **VELVEETA**. Spoon into 13×9-inch baking dish; cover with foil.

BAKE 20 min. Uncover; stir gently. Bake, uncovered, an additional 15 min. or until heated through.

Makes 6 servings, about 1⅓ cups each.

SIZE-WISE:

Need to feed a hungry family of 6? This tasty main dish can be on the table in a matter of minutes!

USE YOUR STOVE:

Brown meat with peppers and onions in large skillet as directed; drain and return to skillet. Add taco seasoning mix, water, potatoes and corn; stir until blended. Cover and cook on medium high heat 5 to 7 min. or until potatoes are tender. Stir in VELVEETA; cook, uncovered, until VELVEETA is completely melted and mixture is well blended, stirring occasionally.

TACO BELL® and HOME ORIGINALS® are trademarks owned and licensed by Taco Bell Corp.

Cheesy Cheeseburger Mac

Prep: 10 min. ● Total: 30 min.

1 lb. ground beef

1¼ cups water

¾ cup milk

⅓ cup ketchup

1 pkg. (12 oz.) **VELVEETA** Shells & Cheese Dinner

1 large tomato, chopped

BROWN meat in large skillet; drain.

ADD water, milk and ketchup; mix well. Bring to boil. Stir in Shell Macaroni; return to boil. Reduce heat to medium-low; cover. Simmer 10 min. or until macaroni is tender.

STIR in Cheese Sauce and tomatoes until well blended. Cook until heated through, stirring occasionally.

Makes 4 servings.

SERVING SUGGESTION:

Serve with a crisp mixed green salad tossed with your favorite KRAFT Dressing.

SUBSTITUTE:

Prepare as directed, substituting 2 pouches (1 cup each) frozen BOCA Meatless Ground Burger for the browned ground beef.

VELVEETA Down-Home Macaroni & Cheese

Prep: 20 min. ● Total: 40 min.

- ¼ cup (½ stick) butter or margarine, divided
- ¼ cup all-purpose flour
- 1 cup milk
- ½ lb. (8 oz.) **VELVEETA** Pasteurized Prepared Cheese Product, cut into ½-inch cubes
- 2 cups elbow macaroni, cooked, drained
- ½ cup **KRAFT** Shredded Cheddar Cheese
- ¼ cup crushed **RITZ** Crackers

PREHEAT oven to 350°F. Melt 3 Tbsp. of the butter in medium saucepan on low heat. Add flour; mix well. Cook 2 min., stirring constantly. Gradually add milk, stirring until well blended. Cook on medium heat until mixture boils and thickens, stirring constantly. Add **VELVEETA**; cook until melted, stirring frequently. Add macaroni; mix lightly.

SPOON into lightly greased 2-qt. casserole dish; sprinkle with shredded cheese. Melt remaining 1 Tbsp. butter; toss with cracker crumbs. Sprinkle over casserole.

BAKE 20 min. or until heated through.

Makes 5 servings, 1 cup each.

HEALTHY LIVING:

Save 60 calories, 9g fat, and 5g saturated fat per serving by preparing with fat-free milk, VELVEETA Made With 2% Milk Reduced Fat Pasteurized Prepared Cheese Product, KRAFT 2% Milk Shredded Reduced Fat Cheddar Cheese and RITZ Reduced Fat Crackers.

JAZZ IT UP:

Stir in ¼ cup OSCAR MAYER Real Bacon Bits with the cooked macaroni.

Creamy Mexican Chicken Pasta

Prep: 10 min. • Total: 25 min.

- 3 cups bow-tie pasta, uncooked
- 1½ boneless, skinless chicken breasts, cut into strips
- ½ lb. (8 oz.) **VELVEETA** Pasteurized Prepared Cheese Product, cut into ½-inch cubes
- 1 can (10¾ oz.) condensed cream of mushroom soup
- 1 cup **TACO BELL® HOME ORIGINALS®** Thick 'N Chunky Salsa
- ¼ cup milk

COOK pasta in large saucepan as directed on package; drain. Return to saucepan.

SPRAY large skillet with nonstick cooking spray. Add chicken; cook and stir 4 to 5 min. or until cooked through.

ADD to pasta in saucepan along with the remaining ingredients; cook on low heat until **VELVEETA** is completely melted and mixture is well blended, stirring occasionally.

Makes 6 servings.

HOW TO CUBE VELVEETA:

Cut measured amount of VELVEETA Pasteurized Prepared Cheese Product into ½-inch-thick slices. Then, cut each slice crosswise in both directions to make cubes.

SUBSTITUTE:

Substitute rotini pasta or any other small shaped pasta for the bow-tie pasta.

SHORTCUT:

Substitute 2 pkg. (6 oz. each) OSCAR MAYER Grilled or Italian Style Chicken Breast Strips for the cooked fresh chicken strips. Cook pasta as directed. Drain; return to same pan. Add chicken breast strips and remaining ingredients; continue as directed.

TACO BELL® and HOME ORIGINALS® are trademarks owned and licensed by Taco Bell Corp.

Hot 'n Hearty Sandwiches

HOT, CHEESY SOUPS AND SANDWICHES
PERFECT FOR PARTY TIME OR ANY TIME

Soups &

VELVEETA BBQ Turkey Griller

Prep: 10 min. • Total: 16 min.

- 8 slices bread
- ¼ lb. (4 oz.) **VELVEETA** Pasteurized Prepared Cheese Product, cut into 8 slices
- 24 slices **OSCAR MAYER** Shaved Smoked Turkey Breast
- ½ of a small onion, sliced, separated into rings
- ¼ cup **BULL'S-EYE** Original Barbecue Sauce
- 8 tsp. margarine, softened

TOP each of 4 of the bread slices with 2 **VELVEETA** slices, 6 turkey slices, 2 or 3 onion rings and 1 Tbsp. barbecue sauce; cover with second bread slice.

SPREAD outsides of sandwiches evenly with margarine.

COOK in skillet on medium heat 3 min. on each side or until golden brown on both sides.

Makes 4 servings, 1 sandwich each.

SUBSTITUTE:
Prepare as directed, using whole-grain bread and VELVEETA Made With 2% Milk Reduced Fat Pasteurized Prepared Cheese Product.

MAKE IT EASY:
For easier slicing of VELVEETA, give the knife blade or cheese slicer's roller bar a light mist of nonstick cooking spray first. No more sticking!

VELVEETA Bacon Burgers

Prep: 10 min. ● Total: 24 min.

1 lb. extra-lean ground beef

2 Tbsp. **KRAFT** Light House Italian Reduced Fat Dressing

¼ lb. (4 oz.) **VELVEETA** Made With 2% Milk Reduced Fat Pasteurized Prepared Cheese Product, cut into 4 slices

4 tsp. **OSCAR MAYER** Real Bacon Recipe Pieces

4 whole wheat hamburger buns, split

SHAPE ground beef into 4 patties. Cook in dressing in skillet on medium-high heat 10 to 12 min. or until burgers are cooked through (160°F), turning after 5 min.

TOP with **VELVEETA** and bacon; cover skillet with lid. Cook an additional 1 to 2 min. or until **VELVEETA** begins to melt.

SERVE in buns.

Makes 4 servings, 1 cheeseburger each.

JAZZ IT UP:

Cover bottom half of each bun with lettuce leaf before topping with burger.

COOK GROUND MEAT THOROUGHLY:

Cook ground beef thoroughly and evenly. The color of the raw ground meat can vary from bright red to light pink. Do not rely on the color of the meat to check for doneness but use an instant read thermometer instead. Ground beef should be cooked to an internal temperature of 160°F.

SERVING SUGGESTION:

Serve with bagged mixed greens tossed with cut-up fresh vegetables. Top with your favorite KRAFT Dressing, such as Light Reduced Fat Ranch.

Santa Fe Chicken Fajita Soup

Prep: 15 min. ● Total: 1 hour 5 min. (incl. refrigerating)

1 pkg. (1.4 oz.) **TACO BELL® HOME ORIGINALS®** Fajita Seasoning
   Mix

⅓ cup water

1 lb. boneless, skinless chicken breasts, cut into thin strips

4 large cloves garlic, minced

2 Tbsp. chopped fresh cilantro

1 large red onion, chopped

1 small green bell pepper, chopped

1 pkg. (8 oz.) **PHILADELPHIA** Fat Free Cream Cheese, cut into cubes

1 lb. (16 oz.) **VELVEETA** Made With 2% Milk Reduced Fat
   Pasteurized Prepared Cheese Product, cut into ½-inch cubes

2 cans (14.5 oz. each) fat-free, reduced-sodium chicken broth

COMBINE seasoning mix and water in medium bowl. Add chicken; toss
until evenly coated. Cover. Refrigerate at least 30 min.

SPRAY large nonstick saucepan with nonstick cooking spray. Add garlic
and cilantro; cook on medium-high heat 1 min. Add chicken mixture,
onions and peppers; mix well. Cook 10 min. or until chicken is cooked
through, stirring frequently.

ADD cream cheese, **VELVEETA** and chicken broth; mix well. Reduce heat
to medium. Cook until cream cheese and **VELVEETA** are completely
melted and chicken mixture is heated through, stirring occasionally.

Makes 8 servings, 1 cup each.

SERVING SUGGESTION:

Serve this hearty main-dish soup with a tossed leafy green salad.

*TACO BELL® and HOME ORIGINALS® are trademarks owned and licensed by Taco Bell
Corp.*

Turkey-Cheese Pita

Prep: 10 min. • Total: 18 min.

 4 whole wheat pita bread rounds

 2 tsp. **GREY POUPON** Hearty Spicy Brown Mustard

16 baby spinach leaves

 ¼ lb. (4 oz.) **VELVEETA** Made With 2% Milk Reduced Fat Pasteurized
    Prepared Cheese Product, sliced, cut into strips

 1 pkg. (6 oz.) **OSCAR MAYER** Thin Sliced Oven Roasted Turkey
    Breast, cut into strips

 ½ cup sliced fresh mushrooms

 ½ cup slivered red onions

SPREAD pita bread evenly with mustard; top *each* with 4 spinach leaves.
Cover with remaining ingredients.

PLACE 1 topped pita on microwaveable plate.

MICROWAVE on HIGH 1 to 2 min. or until **VELVEETA** begins to melt.
Repeat with remaining topped pitas.

Makes 4 servings, 1 topped pita each.

SUBSTITUTE:

Prepare as directed, using your favorite flavor of OSCAR MAYER Thin Sliced
Turkey or Ham.

FUN IDEA:

Prepare as directed. Roll up pitas; tie each with green onion top.

VELVEETA Ultimate Grilled Cheese

Prep: 5 min. ● Total: 11 min.

8 slices white bread

6 oz. **VELVEETA** Pasteurized Prepared Cheese Product, sliced

8 tsp. soft margarine

TOP 4 of the bread slices with **VELVEETA**. Cover with remaining bread slices.

SPREAD outsides of sandwiches evenly with margarine.

COOK in skillet on medium heat 3 min. on each side or until golden brown on both sides.

Makes 4 servings, 1 sandwich each.

SUBSTITUTE:

Prepare as directed, using VELVEETA Made With 2% Milk Reduced Fat Pasteurized Prepared Cheese Product.

Cheesy Spinach Soup

Prep: 15 min. • Total: 25 min.

1 Tbsp. soft reduced calorie margarine

¼ cup chopped onions

2 cups fat-free milk

½ lb. (8 oz.) **VELVEETA** Made With 2% Milk Reduced Fat Pasteurized Prepared Cheese Product, cut into ½-inch cubes

1 pkg. (10 oz.) frozen chopped spinach, cooked, well drained

⅛ tsp. ground nutmeg

dash pepper

MELT margarine in medium saucepan on medium heat. Add onions; cook and stir until tender.

ADD remaining ingredients; cook on low heat until **VELVEETA** is melted and soup is heated through, stirring occasionally.

Makes 4 servings, about 1 cup each.

SIZE-WISE:

Savor the flavor of this cheesy soup while keeping portion size in mind.

SUBSTITUTE:

Prepare as directed, substituting frozen chopped broccoli for the spinach.

USE YOUR MICROWAVE:

Microwave onions and margarine in medium microwavable bowl on HIGH 30 sec. to 1 min. or until onions are tender. Stir in remaining ingredients. Microwave 6 to 8 min. or until VELVEETA is completely melted and soup is heated through, stirring every 3 min.

VELVEETA Salsa Joe Sandwich

Prep: 10 min. ● Total: 25 min.

1 lb. lean ground beef

¼ cup chopped onions

6 oz. **VELVEETA** Pasteurized Prepared Cheese Product, cut into ½-inch cubes

1 cup **TACO BELL® HOME ORIGINALS®** Thick 'N Chunky Salsa

6 kaiser rolls, partially split

BROWN meat with onions in large skillet on medium heat; drain. Return to skillet.

ADD VELVEETA and salsa; mix well. Reduce heat to medium-low; cook until **VELVEETA** is completely melted and mixture is well blended, stirring frequently.

SPOON evenly into rolls just before serving.

Makes 6 servings, 1 sandwich each.

VELVEETA CHEESY TACOS:

Omit rolls. Prepare meat mixture as directed; spoon into 12 TACO BELL® HOME ORIGINALS® Taco Shells. Top with shredded lettuce and chopped tomatoes. Makes 6 servings, 2 tacos each.

JAZZ IT UP:

For extra heat, prepare as directed using VELVEETA Mild Mexican Pasteurized Prepared Cheese Product with Jalapeño Peppers.

CREATIVE LEFTOVERS:

Cover and refrigerate any leftover meat mixture. Reheat, then spoon over split hot baked potatoes.

Cheesy Chicken Ranch Sandwiches

Prep: 5 min. ● Total: 19 min.

- 6 small boneless, skinless chicken breast halves (1½ lb.)
- ⅔ cup **KRAFT** Ranch Dressing, divided
- 6 oz. **VELVEETA** Pasteurized Prepared Cheese Product, sliced
- 6 French bread rolls, split
- 6 large lettuce leaves

PREHEAT broiler. Spray rack of broiler pan with cooking spray; top with chicken. Brush with ⅓ cup of the dressing.

BROIL, 3 to 4 inches from heat, 5 to 6 min. on each side or until chicken is cooked through (165°F). Top with **VELVEETA**. Broil an additional 2 min. or until **VELVEETA** is melted.

SPREAD cut sides of rolls evenly with remaining ⅓ cup dressing; fill with lettuce and chicken.

Makes 6 servings, 1 sandwich each.

SERVING SUGGESTION:

Serve with your favorite fresh fruit.

KEEPING IT SAFE:

Use a visual test to ensure boneless chicken breasts are thoroughly cooked. Cut small slit in thickest part of chicken piece. If meat is totally white with no pink color, it is safe to eat.

STORAGE KNOW-HOW:

Seal chicken in freezer-safe resealable plastic bag. Uncooked chicken can be kept frozen for up to 6 months; cooked chicken for up to 3 months.

Southwestern Corn Soup

Prep: 10 min. ● Total: 25 min.

¾ cup chopped green peppers

1 Tbsp. butter or margarine

3 oz. **PHILADELPHIA** Cream Cheese, cubed

½ lb. (8 oz.) **VELVEETA** Mild Mexican Pasteurized Prepared Cheese Product with Jalapeno Peppers, cut into ½-inch cubes

1 can (14.75 oz.) cream-style corn

1½ cups milk

¼ cup crushed tortilla chips

COOK and stir peppers in butter in medium saucepan on medium heat until crisp-tender. Reduce heat to low.

ADD cream cheese; cook until melted, stirring frequently. Stir in **VELVEETA**, corn and milk. Cook until **VELVEETA** is completely melted and soup is heated through, stirring occasionally.

SERVE topped with the crushed chips.

Makes 6 servings, ¾ cup each.

SERVING SUGGESTION:

Serve with a mixed green salad and slice of whole wheat bread.

USE YOUR MICROWAVE:

Microwave peppers and butter in medium microwavable bowl on HIGH 1 min. or until crisp-tender. Add cream cheese and milk; cover with plastic wrap. Turn back one corner to vent.
Microwave 2 to 3 min. or until cream cheese is melted, stirring after 2 min. Stir in VELVEETA and corn. Microwave 4 to 5 min. or until VELVEETA is completely melted and mixture is well blended, stirring every 2 min.

JAZZ IT UP:

Garnish with chopped cilantro for a burst of extra-fresh flavor.

VELVEETA Sweet & Cheesy Panini

Prep: 10 min. ● Total: 16 min.

- 8 slices bread
- ¼ lb. (4 oz.) **VELVEETA** Pasteurized Prepared Cheese Product, cut into 8 slices
- 24 slices **OSCAR MAYER** Shaved Brown Sugar Ham
- 1 Granny Smith apple, thinly sliced
- 8 tsp. margarine, softened
- 2 tsp. powdered sugar

COVER each of 4 of the bread slices with 2 slices of **VELVEETA**, 6 ham slices and one-fourth of the apples. Top with remaining bread slices.

SPREAD outsides of sandwiches evenly with margarine.

COOK in skillet on medium heat for 3 min. on each side or until **VELVEETA** is melted and sandwiches are golden brown on both sides. Place on serving plates; sprinkle lightly with powdered sugar.

Makes 4 servings, 1 sandwich each.

SUBSTITUTE:

Prepare as directed, using whole grain bread and VELVEETA Made With 2% Milk Reduced Fat Pasteurized Prepared Cheese Product.

NABISCO

Appetizers
& More

Contents

104

144

160

*D*uring the holiday season, parties and family gatherings are all about spending time with the people you love. Whatever holiday you celebrate, food plays an important role in many gatherings.

Most people love to reconnect with family and friends, and planning and preparing the special treats for holiday gatherings provides the opportunity to nurture these special connections. With this in mind, the special food ideas in this booklet can be quickly and easily prepared using familiar ingredients, along with your favorite **NABISCO** Crackers. In *Celebration Starters, Mix 'n Mingle Dips & Spreads,* and *Crowd-Pleasing Cracker Toppings*, you'll find a wide range of easy-to-prepare hearty appetizers, snacks, dips, and spreads. Not only will they satisfy your guests, but they'll also ensure that you won't miss the party yourself! We start with the great flavor and crunch of **TRISCUIT** Crackers, made with 100% whole grains and zero trans fat, **RITZ** Crackers, with their buttery, melt-in-your-mouth flavor and flaky crunch, and the multi-dimensional flavor of **WHEAT THINS** Snack Crackers. Their shapes, flavors, and textures complement the creamy and savory selection of dips, spreads, and toppings perfectly. Furthermore, if looking for better-for-you options, check the nutrition information to find recipes that meet your goals.

We have included some show-stopping desserts in *Tasteful Traditions*, along with simple tips for presenting your food with style and pizzazz. With the goodness of **NILLA** Wafers, **OREO** Chocolate Sandwich Cookies and **HONEY MAID** Honey Grahams, these wonderful family pleasers are deliciously simple. They're perfect for parties since they can be assembled ahead of time and decorated just before serving. Lastly, *Gift-Giving Favorites* is dedicated to the creation of homemade gifts from your very own kitchen. We hope that you enjoy preparing these as much as we enjoyed creating them for you and your family.

As you plan ahead for the holiday season, these recipes can help you entertain with a savvy, sophisticated style while you create lasting memories and have fun at your own parties!

Marianne Arimenta-Dente
Kraft Kitchens

CELEBRATION

Extra-special appetizers for those extra-special holiday gatherings

STARTERS

SHRIMP SPREAD

Prep: 15 min. ● Total: 15 min.

- 1 lb. frozen peeled and deveined shrimp (41 to 50 count), cooked, divided
- 1 pkg. (8 oz.) **PHILADELPHIA** Cream Cheese, softened
- ¾ cup finely chopped celery
- ¼ cup finely chopped stuffed green olives

  RITZ Crackers

CHOP enough shrimp to measure 1 cup; place in medium bowl. Set remaining shrimp aside for later use.

ADD cream cheese, celery and olives to shrimp in bowl; mix well. Spoon onto center of serving plate. Shape into 6-inch round. Arrange remaining shrimp around edge of cream cheese mixture, pressing gently into cream cheese mixture to secure.

SERVE with crackers.

Makes 16 servings, 2 Tbsp. spread and 5 crackers each.

Nutrition Information Per Serving: 160 calories, 10g total fat, 4g saturated fat, 310mg sodium, 11 g carbohydrate, 8g protein.

How to Devein Raw Shrimp:

To devein raw shrimp, remove the outer shell first. Then make a lengthwise shallow cut on the outer curve of the shrimp. (This will expose the black vein.) Loosen the vein with the tip of a sharp knife and then pull with your fingers to completely remove.

SOUTHERN-STYLE CRAB CAKES WITH COOL LIME SAUCE

Prep: 15 min. ● Total: 23 min.

Grated peel and juice from 1 lime, divided

1 cup **KRAFT** Mayo Real Mayonnaise or **MIRACLE WHIP** Dressing, divided

1 env. **GOOD SEASONS** Italian Salad Dressing & Recipe Mix

2 Tbsp. **GREY POUPON** Country Dijon Mustard

2 cans (6 oz. each) crabmeat, drained, flaked

25 **RITZ** Crackers, finely crushed, divided

1 green onion, chopped

¼ cup **BREAKSTONE'S** or **KNUDSEN** Sour Cream

MIX half of the lime juice, ½ cup of the mayo, the salad dressing mix and mustard in medium bowl until well blended. Add crabmeat, ½ cup of the cracker crumbs and the onion; mix lightly.

SHAPE into 18 (½-inch-thick) patties; coat with remaining cracker crumbs.

COOK patties in batches in large nonstick skillet on medium heat 2 min. on each side or until browned on both sides and heated through. Meanwhile, mix remaining ½ cup mayo, remaining lime juice, the lime peel and sour cream until well blended. Serve with crab cakes.

Makes 18 servings, 1 crab cake and 2 tsp. sauce each.

Note: If skillet is not nonstick, cook crab cakes in 1 Tbsp. oil.

Nutrition Information Per Serving: 140 calories, 12g total fat, 2g saturated fat, 340mg sodium, 4g carbohydrate, 4g protein.

Jazz It Up:

Spoon sauce decoratively onto serving plate before topping with crab cake. Garnish with a lime slice and additional chopped green onions.

ROASTED RED PEPPER-BASIL SPREAD

Prep: 15 min. ● Total: 1 hour 15 min. (incl. refrigerating)

1 **tub (12 oz.) PHILADELPHIA** Cream Cheese Spread

¼ cup lightly packed fresh basil leaves

1 clove garlic, peeled

¼ cup drained roasted red peppers

5 pitted black olives, chopped

2 **Tbsp. PLANTERS** Sliced Almonds, toasted

RITZ Crackers

PLACE cream cheese spread in blender; set aside. Wash tub; line with plastic wrap, with ends of wrap extending over side of tub. Set aside.

ADD basil and garlic to cream cheese in blender; cover. Blend using pulsing action until well blended; set aside. Cut a star shape from one of the peppers, using ½-inch star-shaped cutter; set star aside for later use. Chop pepper trimmings and remaining peppers; combine with the olives. Spoon ½ cup of the cream cheese mixture into prepared tub. Cover with the chopped pepper mixture; press lightly into cream cheese mixture. Top with the remaining cream cheese mixture; cover. Refrigerate 1 hour.

UNMOLD cheese spread onto serving plate; remove and discard plastic wrap. Top cheese spread with the almonds and pepper star. Serve as a spread with the crackers.

Makes 1½ cups or 12 servings, 2 Tbsp. spread and 5 crackers each.

Make Ahead: Prepare cheese spread as directed. Cover and refrigerate up to 24 hours. Unmold and continue as directed.

Nutrition Information Per Serving: 180 calories, 13g total fat, 6g saturated fat, 300mg sodium, 12g carbohydrate, 3g protein.

Jazz It Up:

For a holiday flair, serve with **RITZ SIMPLY SOCIALS** Crackers.

EASY RITZ HOT WINGS

Prep: 20 min. ● Total: 1 hour

- **1 sleeve RITZ Crackers (38 crackers), finely crushed**
- **1 tsp. dried oregano leaves**
- **½ tsp. garlic powder**
- **½ tsp. paprika**
- **⅛ tsp. coarsely ground black pepper**
- **2 lb. chicken wings, separated at joints, tips discarded**
- **½ cup hot pepper sauce**

PREHEAT oven to 350°F. Mix cracker crumbs and seasonings in shallow dish.

COAT chicken with hot pepper sauce, then dip in crumb mixture, turning to evenly coat both sides of each wing piece. Place in single layer on greased baking sheet.

BAKE 35 to 40 min. or until golden brown and cooked through (165°F), turning pieces over after 20 min. Serve warm.

Makes 20 servings, about 1 chicken wing each.

Nutrition Information Per Serving: 120 calories, 7g total fat, 2g saturated fat, 160mg sodium, 4g carbohydrate, 8g protein.

Serving Suggestion:

Serve these flavorful appetizers with vegetable sticks and **KRAFT ROKA** Blue Cheese Dressing.

CRANBERRY AND PECAN CHEESE LOG

Prep: 15 min. ● Total: 45 min. (incl. refrigerating)

1 container (8 oz.) **PHILADELPHIA** Light Cream Cheese Spread

¼ cup chopped dried cranberries

1 Tbsp. grated orange peel

½ cup coarsely chopped **PLANTERS** Pecans, toasted

   TRISCUIT Rosemary & Olive Oil Crackers

MIX cream cheese spread, cranberries and orange peel until well blended. Shape into 6-inch log.

ROLL in pecans until evenly coated on all sides. Wrap tightly in plastic wrap.

REFRIGERATE at least 30 min. Serve as a spread with the crackers.

Makes 1½ cups or 12 servings, 2 Tbsp. spread and 6 crackers each.

Nutrition Information Per Serving: 200 calories, 10g total fat, 2.5g saturated fat, 220mg sodium, 24g carbohydrate, 5g protein.

Take Along:

Bringing this colorful cheese log to a holiday party? Remember to pack a copy of the recipe. You're sure to get requests!

SHALLOT & BACON BRIE

Prep: 10 min. ● Total: 11 min.

2 slices **OSCAR MAYER** Bacon

2 shallots, thinly sliced

2 tsp. **GREY POUPON** Savory Honey Mustard

1 wheel Brie cheese (8 oz.)

RITZ Crackers

COOK bacon in nonstick skillet on medium heat until crisp. Drain bacon, reserving drippings in skillet; set bacon aside.

ADD shallots to bacon drippings in skillet; cook until shallots are tender, stirring frequently. Crumble bacon into small bowl. Add shallot mixture and mustard; mix well. Spoon over cheese in microwaveable serving dish.

MICROWAVE on HIGH 45 sec. or just until cheese is warmed. Serve as a spread with the crackers.

Makes 16 servings, 2 Tbsp. spread and 5 crackers each.

Nutrition Information Per Serving: 150 calories, 10g total fat, 4g saturated fat, 270mg sodium, 12g carbohydrate, 5g protein.

The Perfect Cheese Tray:

Cheese trays are ideal for entertaining. Be sure to include a selection of KRAFT Cheeses in mild, medium and strong flavors. Cut cheeses into an assortment of shapes, then arrange on a large tray or platter along with a sampling of NABISCO crackers and colorful fresh fruit.

THE ULTIMATE STUFFED MUSHROOM

Prep: 20 min. ● Total: 35 min.

20 mushrooms

3 Tbsp. butter

2 Tbsp. finely chopped onions

2 Tbsp. finely chopped red peppers

14 **RITZ** Crackers, finely crushed (about ½ cup crumbs)

2 Tbsp. **KRAFT** 100% Grated Parmesan Cheese

½ tsp. Italian seasoning

PREHEAT oven to 400°F. Remove stems from mushrooms. Finely chop enough of the stems to measure ¼ cup; set aside. Cover and refrigerate remaining stems for other use.

MELT butter in large skillet on medium heat. Add ¼ cup chopped mushroom stems, the onions and peppers; cook and stir until vegetables are tender. Stir in cracker crumbs, cheese and Italian seasoning. Spoon crumb mixture evenly into mushroom caps. Place on baking sheet.

BAKE 15 min. or until heated through.

Makes 20 servings, 1 stuffed mushroom each.

Make Ahead: Mushrooms can be stuffed several hours in advance. Cover and refrigerate until ready to serve. Uncover and bake at 400°F for 20 min. or until heated through.

Nutrition Information Per Serving: 35 calories, 2.5g total fat, 1g saturated fat, 45mg sodium, 2g carbohydrate, 1g protein.

Make It Easy:

When preparing mushrooms for stuffing, use a melon baller to carefully scoop a little mushroom flesh from the cap after removing the stem. Then use the melon baller to easily scoop the filling mixture into the mushrooms.

ROASTED EGGPLANT CAPONATA

Prep: 1 hour 10 min. ● Total: 3 hours 10 min. (incl. refrigerating)

1 head garlic

1 Tbsp. olive oil

1 large eggplant (1½ lb.)

1 can (14½ oz.) diced tomatoes, drained

¼ cup chopped fresh parsley

2 Tbsp. chopped red onions

2 Tbsp. balsamic vinegar

¼ tsp. salt

1 Tbsp. KRAFT Shredded Parmesan Cheese

WHEAT THINS Snack Crackers

PREHEAT oven to 375°F. Cut ½-inch-thick slice off top of garlic, exposing cloves; discard top. Brush cut-side of garlic lightly with oil; wrap tightly in foil. Place on ungreased baking sheet. Pierce eggplant in several places with fork or sharp knife. Place on baking sheet with garlic. Bake 50 min. to 1 hour or until both are tender; cool slightly.

PEEL eggplant; cut into small pieces. Place in medium bowl. Mince 3 of the garlic cloves. Add to eggplant along with the tomatoes, parsley, onions, vinegar and salt; mix well. Cover; refrigerate at least 2 hours. Meanwhile, store remaining garlic in refrigerator for another use.

SPRINKLE eggplant mixture with cheese just before serving. Serve as a dip with the crackers.

Makes 2 cups or 16 servings, 2 Tbsp. dip and 16 crackers each.

How to Serve Warm: Just before serving, spoon the dip into microwaveable bowl. Microwave on HIGH 1 min., stirring after 30 sec.

Nutrition Information Per Serving: 170 calories, 7g total fat, 1g saturated fat, 320mg sodium, 24g carbohydrate, 3g protein.

Creative Leftovers:

Store leftover roasted garlic in tightly covered container in refrigerator. Spread onto your favorite **NABISCO** Crackers, then top with any leftover eggplant mixture.

MARINATED FETA CHEESE

Prep: 10 min. ● Total: 1 hour 10 min. (incl. refrigerating)

- 1 pkg. (8 oz.) **ATHENOS** Traditional Feta Cheese
- 2 Tbsp. **GOOD SEASONS** Italian Vinaigrette with Extra Virgin Olive Oil Dressing
- 1 tsp. finely chopped fennel tops
- 1 tsp. finely chopped fresh rosemary
- ¼ tsp. crushed red pepper
- ¼ tsp. grated lemon peel

CUT cheese into 32 cubes; place in medium bowl.

ADD remaining ingredients; mix lightly. Cover.

REFRIGERATE at least 1 hour.

Makes 8 servings, 4 cheese cubes each.

Make Ahead: Cheese mixture can be refrigerated up to 24 hours before serving.

Nutrition Information Per Serving (cheese only): 80 calories, 7g total fat, 4.5g saturated fat, 360mg sodium, 1g carbohydrate, 5g protein.

Serving Suggestion:

Serve with SOCIABLES Savory Crackers, RITZ Snowflake Crackers or RITZ SIMPLY SOCIALS Crackers.

MIX 'N MINGLE DIPS &

Make these recipes ahead
of time and enjoy the
party with your guests!

SPREADS

LAYERED PESTO AND RED PEPPER DIP

Prep: 15 min. ● Total: 1 hour 15 min.
(incl. refrigerating)

- 1 tub (8 oz.) **PHILADELPHIA** Light Cream Cheese Spread, divided
- ¼ cup chopped drained roasted red peppers
- 1 Tbsp. pesto
- 1 Tbsp. milk

   WHEAT THINS Snack Crackers

PLACE half of the cream cheese spread and the peppers in blender; cover. Blend 30 to 40 sec. or until well blended, stopping and scraping down side of blender as needed.

MIX remaining cream cheese spread, pesto and milk until well blended. Spread onto small serving plate; top with the red pepper mixture. Cover.

REFRIGERATE at least 1 hour before serving.

Makes about 1 cup or 9 servings, 2 Tbsp. dip and 16 crackers each.

Make Ahead: The 2 layers of dip can be made up to 1 day ahead and stored in separate tightly covered containers in the refrigerator. For best results, layer the dips no more than 2 hours before serving.

Nutrition Information Per Serving: 210 calories, 10g total fat, 3g saturated fat, 420mg sodium, 23g carbohydrate, 5g protein.

HOT APPLE PIE DIP

Prep: 10 min. ● Total: 22 min.

- 1 tub (8 oz.) **PHILADELPHIA** Light Cream Cheese Spread
- 2 Tbsp. brown sugar
- ½ tsp. pumpkin pie spice
- 1 apple, chopped, divided
- ¼ cup **KRAFT** 2% Milk Shredded Reduced Fat Cheddar Cheese
- 1 Tbsp. finely chopped **PLANTERS** Pecan Pieces

   WHEAT THINS Lightly Cinnamon Snack Crackers

PREHEAT oven to 375°F. Mix cream cheese spread, sugar and spice in medium bowl until well blended. Stir in half of the chopped apple.

SPREAD into 8-inch pie plate or small casserole dish. Top with remaining apples, the Cheddar cheese and pecans.

BAKE 10 to 12 min. or until heated through. Serve with the crackers.

Makes 2 cups or 16 servings, 2 Tbsp. dip and 15 crackers each.

Substitute: Substitute ground cinnamon for the pumpkin pie spice.

Nutrition Information Per Serving: 190 calories, 8g total fat, 2.5g saturated fat, 210mg sodium, 25g carbohydrate, 4g protein.

LAYERED HOT ARTICHOKE AND FETA DIP

Prep: 10 min. ● Total: 30 min.

1 pkg. (8 oz.) **PHILADELPHIA** Neufchâtel Cheese, ⅓ Less Fat than Cream Cheese, softened

1 can (14 oz.) artichoke hearts, drained, chopped

½ cup **KRAFT** Shredded Parmesan Cheese

2 cloves garlic, minced

1 small red pepper, chopped

1 pkg. (3.5 oz.) **ATHENOS** Crumbled Reduced Fat Feta Cheese

1 Tbsp. sliced black olives

   WHEAT THINS Toasted Chips Multi-Grain

PREHEAT oven to 350°F. Mix Neufchâtel cheese, artichokes, Parmesan cheese and garlic until well blended.

SPREAD into 3-cup ovenproof serving dish; top with peppers and feta cheese.

BAKE 20 min.; top with olives. Serve with the chips.

Makes 3 cups or 24 servings, 2 Tbsp. dip and 15 chips each.

Make Ahead: Assemble dip as directed; cover and refrigerate up to 8 hours. When ready to serve, uncover and bake at 350°F for 25 min. or until heated through.

Nutrition Information Per Serving: 170 calories, 7g total fat, 2.5g saturated fat, 500mg sodium, 22g carbohydrate, 5g protein.

CHUNKY VEGETABLE HUMMUS

Prep: 10 min. ● Total: 10 min.

1 container (7 oz.) **ATHENOS** Original Hummus

¾ cup chopped, peeled and seeded cucumbers

¼ cup chopped red onions

1 plum tomato, chopped

¼ cup **ATHENOS** Traditional Crumbled Feta Cheese

WHEAT THINS Big Snack Crackers

SPREAD hummus onto serving plate.

TOP with layers of cucumbers, onions and tomatoes; sprinkle with cheese.

SERVE with the crackers.

Makes 2½ cups or 20 servings, 2 Tbsp. dip and 11 crackers each.

Substitute: Prepare as directed, using **ATHENOS** Crumbled Reduced Fat Feta Cheese.

Nutrition Information Per Serving: 170 calories, 7g total fat, 1.5g saturated fat, 350mg sodium, 24g carbohydrate, 3g protein.

Shortcut:

Save time by preparing with already-chopped vegetables purchased at the salad bar in your local supermarket.

HOT LAYERED BUFFALO SPREAD

Prep: 10 min. ● Total: 12 min.

1 pkg. (8 oz.) **PHILADELPHIA** Cream Cheese, softened

1 cup chopped cooked chicken

1 Tbsp. hot pepper sauce

½ cup **ATHENOS** Crumbled Blue Cheese

2 Tbsp. chopped red bell peppers

RITZ Crackers and celery sticks

SPREAD cream cheese onto microwaveable plate or bottom of 9-inch pie plate.

TOSS chicken with hot sauce; spoon over cream cheese. Top with blue cheese and peppers.

MICROWAVE on HIGH 1½ to 2 min. or until heated through. Serve with crackers and celery.

Makes about 2½ cups spread or 20 servings,
2 Tbsp. spread, 5 crackers and 5 celery sticks each.

Substitute: Substitute chopped **OSCAR MAYER** Southwestern Seasoned Chicken Breast Strips for the chopped cooked chicken.

Nutrition Information Per Serving: 150 calories, 9g total fat, 4g saturated fat, 250mg sodium, 11 g carbohydrate, 5g protein.

PINECONE CHEESE SPREAD

Prep: 20 min. ● Total: 2 hours 35 min. (incl. refrigerating)

- 1 pkg. (8 oz.) **PHILADELPHIA** Cream Cheese, softened
- 1 pkg. (8 oz.) **KRAFT** 2% Milk Shredded Reduced Fat Four Cheese Mexican Style Cheese
- 2 Tbsp. **GREY POUPON** Dijon Mustard
- 2 Tbsp. chopped canned green chilies
- ⅓ cup **PLANTERS** Sliced Almonds, toasted

  RITZ Crackers

PLACE cream cheese, shredded cheese and mustard in food processor or blender; cover. Process until well blended. Stir in chilies.

PLACE on sheet of waxed paper; shape into 4-inch oval to resemble a pinecone. Insert almonds in rows to completely cover cream cheese mixture; cover.

REFRIGERATE 2 hours or until firm. Let stand at room temperature 15 min. before serving with the crackers.

> *Makes 2 cups or 16 servings, 2 Tbsp. spread and 5 crackers each.*

Make Ahead: Spread can be stored, tightly covered, in refrigerator up to 5 days.

Substitute: Serve with **RITZ** Snowflake Crackers.

Nutrition Information Per Serving: 190 calories, 13g total fat, 6g saturated fat, 360mg sodium, 11 g carbohydrate, 6g protein.

Jazz It Up:

Prepare as directed, adding 1 tsp. hot pepper sauce to the cream cheese mixture before shaping as directed.

HOT HOLIDAY BROCCOLI DIP

Prep: 10 min. ● Total: 40 min.

- **1 cup MIRACLE WHIP Light Dressing**
- **1 pkg. (10 oz.) frozen chopped broccoli, thawed, well drained**
- **1 jar (2 oz.) diced pimientos, drained**
- **½ cup KRAFT 100% Grated Parmesan Cheese**
- **1 cup KRAFT 2% Milk Shredded Reduced Fat Mozzarella Cheese, divided**
- **WHEAT THINS Snack Crackers**

PREHEAT oven to 350°F. Combine dressing, broccoli, pimientos, Parmesan cheese and ½ cup of the mozzarella cheese.

SPREAD into baking dish or 9-inch pie plate.

BAKE 20 to 25 min. or until heated through. Sprinkle with remaining ½ cup mozzarella cheese. Bake an additional 5 min. or until mozzarella cheese is melted. Serve with the crackers.

Makes about 3 cups or 25 servings, about 2 Tbsp. dip and 16 crackers each.

Nutrition Information Per Serving: 180 calories, 8g total fat, 2g saturated fat, 440mg sodium, 23g carbohydrate, 5g protein.

Time-Out:

Take a time-out during the busy holiday season to watch a movie or two! Pick a holiday classic or something that's guaranteed to make you laugh. Prepare your favorite snack and enjoy!

CHEESY HOT CRAB AND RED PEPPER DIP

Prep: 10 min. • Total: 30 min.

1½ cups **KRAFT** 2% Milk Shredded Reduced Fat Mozzarella Cheese, divided

1 pkg. (8 oz.) **PHILADELPHIA** Neufchâtel Cheese, ⅓ Less Fat than Cream Cheese, softened

1 tsp. garlic powder

1 tsp. Italian seasoning

1 medium red pepper, chopped

1 small onion, finely chopped

1 can (6 oz.) crabmeat, drained

WHEAT THINS Snack Crackers

PREHEAT oven to 375°F. Remove ½ cup of the mozzarella cheese; cover and refrigerate until ready to use. Mix all remaining ingredients except crackers until well blended.

SPREAD into 9-inch pie plate.

BAKE 20 min. or until crab mixture is heated through and top is lightly browned. Sprinkle with reserved ½ cup mozzarella cheese. Serve hot with the crackers.

Makes 3 cups or 24 servings, 2 Tbsp. dip and 16 crackers each.

Substitute: Prepare as directed, using **PHILADELPHIA** Cream Cheese and **KRAFT** Shredded Mozzarella Cheese. Serve with **WHEAT THINS** Toasted Chips Multi-Grain or **RITZ** Toasted Chips.

Nutrition Information Per Serving: 200 calories, 9g total fat, 3g saturated fat, 380mg sodium, 22g carbohydrate, 7g protein.

APPLE, PECAN & BLUE CHEESE SPREAD

Prep: 10 min. ● Total: 2 hours 10 min. (incl. refrigerating)

- **1** container (8 oz.) **PHILADELPHIA** Light Cream Cheese Spread
- **½** cup **BREAKSTONE'S** Reduced Fat or **KNUDSEN** Light Sour Cream
- **1** Rome Beauty apple, finely chopped
- **¼** cup **ATHENOS** Crumbled Blue Cheese
- **¼** cup chopped red onion
- **¼** cup chopped toasted **PLANTERS** Pecans
  TRISCUIT Crackers

BEAT cream cheese spread and sour cream in medium bowl until well blended.

ADD apples, blue cheese, onions and pecans; mix well. Cover.

REFRIGERATE at least 2 hours. Serve as a spread with the crackers.

Makes 3 cups or 24 servings, 2 Tbsp. spread and 6 crackers each.

Nutrition Information Per Serving: 170 calories, 8g total fat, 2.5g saturated fat, 250mg sodium, 22g carbohydrate, 4g protein.

Serving Suggestion:

For a unique dip container, cut top off and hollow out a large red apple. Stand upright on serving platter and fill with dip just before serving. Surround with crackers.

CHEESY CHRISTMAS TREE

Prep: 10 min. ● Total: 10 min.

1 pkg. (8 oz.) **PHILADELPHIA** Cream Cheese

½ cup pesto

¼ cup chopped red peppers

1 stick **KRAFT POLLY-O TWIST-UMS** String Cheese

RITZ Crackers

CUT block of cream cheese diagonally in half. Arrange both halves, with points together, on serving plate to resemble Christmas-tree shape.

CUT a 2-inch piece from the string cheese. Place at bottom of tree for the trunk. Wrap up remaining string cheese; refrigerate until ready to use for snacking or other use.

SPOON pesto over cream cheese; sprinkle with peppers. Serve as a spread with the crackers.

Makes 1½ cups or 12 servings, 2 Tbsp. spread and 5 crackers each.

Substitute: Prepare as directed, using **PHILADELPHIA** Neufchâtel Cheese, ⅓ Less Fat than Cream Cheese.

Nutrition Information Per Serving: 200 calories, 16g total fat, 6g saturated fat, 280mg sodium, 12g carbohydrate, 3g protein.

CROWD-PLEASING
CRACKER

Perfect pairings of crunchy crackers
and special toppings for
your most elegant gatherings

TOPPINGS

"BRUSCHETTA" TRISCUIT

Prep: 10 min. ● Total: 10 min.

- 1 small tomato, finely chopped (about ½ cup)
- ¼ cup **KRAFT** 2% Milk Shredded Reduced Fat Mozzarella Cheese
- 3 Tbsp. sliced green onions
- 1 Tbsp. **KRAFT** Light Zesty Italian Reduced Fat Dressing
- 40 **TRISCUIT** Crackers
- 1 pkg. (8 oz.) **PHILADELPHIA** Neufchâtel Cheese, ⅓ Less Fat than Cream Cheese, softened

MIX tomatoes, cheese, onions and dressing.

SPREAD each cracker with about 1 tsp. of the Neufchâtel cheese; top with 1 tsp. of the tomato mixture.

Makes 20 servings, 2 topped crackers each.

Make Ahead: Prepare tomato mixture as directed. Add Neufchâtel cheese; mix well. Cover and refrigerate up to 24 hours. Spread onto crackers just before serving.

Nutrition Information Per Serving: 70 calories, 4.5g total fat, 2g saturated fat, 130mg sodium, 7g carbohydrate, 2g protein.

CAPRESE TOPPER

Prep: 5 min. ● Total: 12 min.

 4 oz. **POLLY-O** Part Skim Mozzarella Cheese, cut into 9 slices

18 **TRISCUIT** Fire Roasted Tomato & Olive Oil Crackers

 2 plum tomatoes, cut into 9 slices each

 1 Tbsp. pesto

18 small fresh basil leaves

PREHEAT oven to 350°F. Cut each cheese slice in half.

TOP crackers with cheese and tomatoes. Place on baking sheet.

BAKE 5 to 7 min. or until cheese is melted. Top with pesto and basil. Serve warm.

Makes 1½ doz. or 9 servings, 2 topped crackers each.

Serving Suggestion: When serving appetizers, offer a variety of colors, shapes and flavors. Include an assortment of dips, cracker toppers and spreads in both hot and cold forms.

Nutrition Information Per Serving: 90 calories, 4.5g total fat, 2g saturated fat, 160mg sodium, 8g carbohydrate, 5g protein.

SHRIMP APPETIZERS WITH GREEN MAYONNAISE

Prep: 20 min. ● Total: 1 hour 20 min. (incl. refrigerating)

¼ cup **KRAFT** Mayo Light Mayonnaise

2 Tbsp. minced fresh parsley

1 Tbsp. finely chopped green onion

½ tsp. grated lime peel

18 shrimp (31 to 40 count), cleaned, cooked

18 **WHEAT THINS** Big Snack Crackers

MIX mayo, parsley, onion and lime peel in medium bowl. Add shrimp; toss to evenly coat. Cover.

REFRIGERATE at least 1 hour.

SPOON onto crackers just before serving.

Makes 1½ doz. or 6 servings, 3 topped crackers each.

Substitute: Prepare as directed, using **RITZ** Crackers or **TRISCUIT** Crackers.

Shrimp Sizes: The size of a shrimp is indicated by the number of shrimp per pound. The smaller the number, the larger the shrimp. Less than 15 is jumbo shrimp; 16 to 20 is extra-large shrimp; 21 to 30 is large shrimp; and 31 to 40 is medium shrimp.

Nutrition Information Per Serving (without garnish): 90 calories, 5g total fat, 1g saturated fat, 190mg sodium, 7g carbohydrate, 3g protein.

Jazz It Up:

Top each appetizer with small strips of roasted red peppers and a parsley sprig.

ARTICHOKE-CHEESE PUFFS

Prep: 10 min. ● Total: 50 min. (incl. refrigerating)

36 RITZ Crackers, divided

1 pkg. (8 oz.) **PHILADELPHIA** Cream Cheese, softened

¼ cup **KRAFT** 100% Grated Parmesan Cheese

¼ cup **KRAFT** 2% Milk Shredded Reduced Fat Mozzarella Cheese

½ cup chopped drained canned artichoke hearts

CRUSH 4 of the crackers. Place in shallow dish; set aside. Mix cheeses and artichokes until well blended. Shape 2 tsp. of the cheese mixture into ball. (If cheese mixture is too soft, cover and refrigerate until firm enough to shape into ball.) Repeat with remaining cheese mixture to make a total of 32 balls. Roll in cracker crumbs until evenly coated. Place in single layer on wax paper-covered tray; cover. Refrigerate 30 min.

PREHEAT oven to 350°F. Arrange remaining 32 crackers in single layer on baking sheet; top each with 1 cheese ball.

BAKE 10 min. or until heated through.

Makes 16 servings, 2 cheese puffs each.

Shortcut: Serve these delicious appetizers cold. Prepare cheese balls as directed and refrigerate up to 24 hours. Place 1 cheese ball on each cracker just before serving.

Substitute: Prepare as directed, using **RITZ** Snowflake Crackers.

Nutrition Information Per Serving (with cracker crumb coating): 100 calories, 8g total fat, 4g saturated fat, 200mg sodium, 6g carbohydrate, 3g protein.

Jazz It Up:

Try adding one of the following to the cracker crumbs: toasted sesame seeds; chopped fresh dill or fresh chives; finely chopped red, green and yellow peppers. Or omit the crumbs and coat only in the alternative coating.

RED ONION-BALSAMIC TOPPER

Prep: 10 min. ● Total: 52 min.

- **1** Tbsp. olive oil
- **1** red onion, thinly sliced (about 1 cup)
- **2** Tbsp. balsamic vinegar
- **48** **TRISCUIT** Rosemary & Olive Oil Crackers
- **¼** cup **BREAKSTONE'S** Reduced Fat or **KNUDSEN** Light Sour Cream

HEAT oil in large skillet on medium heat. Add onions; cook 10 min. or until tender, stirring frequently. Stir in vinegar; cook an additional 1 to 2 min. or until vinegar is evaporated. Cool.

SPOON 1 tsp. of the onion mixture onto each cracker; top with ¼ tsp. of the sour cream.

SERVE warm.

Makes 4 doz. or 16 servings, 3 topped crackers each.

Creative Leftovers: For a heartier appetizer, top each cracker with a thin slice of leftover cooked steak before covering with the onion mixture and sour cream.

Nutrition Information Per Serving: 80 calories, 3.5g total fat, 0.5g saturated fat, 70mg sodium, 11g carbohydrate, 2g protein.

Jazz It Up:

Garnish topped crackers with chopped fresh parsley.

TUSCAN CHICKEN BITES

Prep: 15 min. ● Total: 1 hour 15 min. (incl. refrigerating)

1 small boneless, skinless chicken breast half (4 oz.), cooked, finely chopped (about ¾ cup)

¼ cup **BREAKSTONE'S FREE** or **KNUDSEN FREE** Fat Free Sour Cream

2 green onions, finely chopped

2 Tbsp. finely chopped roasted red peppers

1 tsp. grated lemon peel

½ tsp. chopped fresh rosemary

24 **TRISCUIT** Cracked Pepper & Olive Oil Crackers

24 baby arugula leaves

COMBINE all ingredients except crackers and arugula; cover.

REFRIGERATE at least 1 hour.

TOP each cracker with 1 arugula leaf and 2 tsp. of the chicken mixture just before serving.

Makes 2 doz. or 8 servings, 3 topped crackers each.

Substitute: Prepare as directed, substituting 2 small marinated sun-dried tomatoes, finely chopped, for the roasted red peppers.

Nutrition Information Per Serving: 90 calories, 2.5g total fat, 0g saturated fat, 105mg sodium, 12g carbohydrate, 5g protein.

RITZ CHEESY-CRAB TOPPER

Prep: 10 min. ● Total: 1 hour 10 min. (incl. refrigerating)

 4 oz. (½ of 8 oz. pkg.) **PHILADELPHIA** Cream Cheese, softened

 ¼ cup **BREAKSTONE'S** or **KNUDSEN** Sour Cream

 1 can (6 oz.) crabmeat, drained, flaked

 ¼ cup chopped fresh parsley

 1 Tbsp. **KRAFT** 100% Grated Parmesan Cheese

 3 drops hot pepper sauce

48 **RITZ** Crackers

MIX all ingredients except crackers; cover.

REFRIGERATE at least 1 hour.

SPOON about 1 tsp. of the crabmeat mixture onto each cracker just before serving.

Makes 4 doz. or 16 servings, 3 topped crackers each.

Substitute: Don't have canned crabmeat? Use 1 (6 oz.) can white tuna in water instead.

Nutrition Information Per Serving: 90 calories, 6g total fat, 2.5g saturated fat, 140mg sodium, 7g carbohydrate, 3g protein.

ROAST BEEF, ARUGULA AND BLUE CHEESE TOPPERS

Prep: 10 min. ● Total: 10 min.

12 **TRISCUIT** Rosemary & Olive Oil Crackers

12 baby arugula leaves

3 thin slices deli roast beef (about 2½ oz.), quartered

1 Tbsp. **KRAFT** Light **ROKA** Blue Cheese Reduced Fat Dressing

3 grape or cherry tomatoes, quartered

TOP crackers with remaining ingredients.

SERVE immediately.

Makes 1 doz. or 4 servings, 3 topped crackers each.

Substitute: Prepare as directed, using thinly sliced leftover cooked roast beef or steak.

Nutrition Information Per Serving: 110 calories, 4g total fat, 1g saturated fat, 120mg sodium, 11g carbohydrate, 7g protein.

MANDARIN ALMOND-CHICKEN BITES

Prep: 10 min. ● Total: 1 hour 10 min. (incl. refrigerating)

- ½ **cup finely chopped cooked chicken**
- ½ **cup drained canned mandarin orange segments, chopped**
- ¼ **cup dried cranberries**
- 2 **Tbsp. PLANTERS Sliced Almonds**
- 2 **Tbsp. MIRACLE WHIP Light Dressing**
- 48 **TRISCUIT Crackers**

MIX chicken, oranges, cranberries, almonds and dressing; cover.

REFRIGERATE at least 1 hour.

TOP each cracker with 1 tsp. of the chicken mixture just before serving.

Makes 4 doz. or 16 servings, 3 topped crackers each.

Make Ahead: Chicken mixture can be stored in refrigerator up to 24 hours before spooning onto crackers as directed.

Nutrition Information Per Serving: 90 calories, 3.5g total fat, 0.5g saturated fat, 110mg sodium, 12g carbohydrate, 3g protein.

Jazz It Up:

Garnish topped crackers with a parsley sprig.

RITZ HOLIDAY BELL

Prep: 10 min. • Total: 10 min.

 6 slices **OSCAR MAYER** Hard Salami
 1 pkg. (6 oz.) **KRAFT** Cracker Cuts Mild Cheddar Cheese
18 **RITZ** Crackers
18 thin red pepper strips
 2 tsp. chopped fresh parsley

CUT 3 small bell-shaped pieces out of each salami slice and 1 small bell-shaped piece out of each cheese slice, using small cookie cutter or sharp knife.

TOP crackers with salami and cheese.

DECORATE with the peppers and parsley.

Makes 1½ doz. or 6 servings, 3 topped crackers each.

Fun Idea: Not sure what to do with the cheese after the cutouts are removed from the cheese slices? Fill them with additional salami bells and place on top of additional **RITZ** Crackers.

Nutrition Information Per Serving: 120 calories, 9g total fat, 4g saturated fat, 260mg sodium, 6g carbohydrate, 5g protein.

Jazz It Up:

Use a variety of small, holiday-shaped cookie cutters such as trees, ornaments and stars for a festive look.

TASTEFUL TRADITIONS

Classic desserts made better by adding
your favorite cookies "all dressed up"

EASY CHOCOLATE ÉCLAIR SQUARES

Prep: 30 min. ● Total: 3 hours 30 min. (incl. refrigerating)

- **2** cups cold milk, divided
- **1** pkg. (4-serving size) **JELL-O** Vanilla Flavor Instant Pudding & Pie Filling
- **1** tub (8 oz.) **COOL WHIP** Whipped Topping, thawed
- **22** **HONEY MAID** Honey Grahams
- **4** squares **BAKER'S** Unsweetened Baking Chocolate
- **¼** cup (½ stick) butter or margarine
- **1½** cups powdered sugar

POUR 1¾ cups of the milk into large bowl. Add dry pudding mix. Beat with wire whisk 2 min. Gently stir in whipped topping. Layer one-third of the grahams and half of the whipped topping mixture in 13×9-inch pan, breaking grahams as necessary to fit; repeat layers. Top with remaining grahams.

MICROWAVE chocolate and butter in medium microwaveable bowl on HIGH 1½ min., stirring after 1 min. Stir until chocolate is completely melted. Add sugar and remaining ¼ cup milk; stir until well blended. Immediately spread over grahams.

REFRIGERATE at least 4 hours or overnight. Store any leftover dessert in refrigerator.

Makes 24 servings, 1 square each.

Nutrition Information Per Serving: 180 calories, 8g total fat, 5g saturated fat, 170mg sodium, 27g carbohydrate, 2g protein.

Latte Éclair Squares:

Prepare as directed, substituting ¾ cup chilled, brewed, double-strength MAXWELL HOUSE Coffee for ¾ cup of the milk used to prepare the pudding.

RITZ ANGEL PIE

Prep: 15 min. ● Total: 45 min.

- **3** egg whites
- **½** tsp. vanilla
- **1** cup sugar
- **24** **RITZ** Crackers, finely crushed (about 1 cup)
- **1** cup finely chopped **PLANTERS** Pecans
- **¼** tsp. **CALUMET** Baking Powder
- **1½** cups thawed **COOL WHIP** Whipped Topping

PREHEAT oven to 350°F. Beat egg whites in large bowl with electric mixer on high speed until soft peaks form. Blend in vanilla. Gradually add sugar, beating after each addition until well blended. Continue to beat until stiff peaks form. Mix cracker crumbs, pecans and baking powder. Add to egg white mixture; stir gently until well blended. Spread into greased 9-inch pie plate.

BAKE 30 min. Cool completely.

TOP with the whipped topping just before serving. Store any leftover dessert in refrigerator.

Makes 8 servings, 1 slice each.

Nutrition Information Per Serving (with raspberry sauce): 310 calories, 16g total fat, 4g saturated fat, 125mg sodium, 41g carbohydrate, 4g protein.

Jazz It Up:

Toss 1½ cups (about half of 12 oz. pkg.) frozen raspberries with 2 tsp. sugar in microwaveable bowl. Microwave on HIGH 30 sec.; stir until raspberries are thawed and sugar is dissolved. Place in blender; cover. Blend until smooth. Strain to remove seeds, if desired. Drizzle over pie just before serving. Garnish with a few fresh raspberries.

WHITE & BLACK-TIE-AFFAIR PIE

Prep: 30 min. ● Total: 5 hours (incl. refrigerating)

57 NILLA Wafers, divided

2 Tbsp. sugar

¼ cup (½ stick) butter or margarine, melted

2 cups cold milk, divided

1 pkg. (4-serving size) JELL-O White Chocolate Flavor Instant Pudding & Pie Filling

1 tub (8 oz.) COOL WHIP Whipped Topping, thawed

1 pkg. (4-serving size) JELL-O Chocolate Flavor Instant Pudding & Pie Filling

2 squares BAKER'S Semi-Sweet Baking Chocolate

CRUSH 35 of the wafers. Mix crumbs with sugar and butter until well blended. Press firmly onto bottom and up side of 9-inch pie plate. Pour 1 cup of the milk into medium bowl. Add dry white chocolate flavor pudding mix. Beat with wire whisk 2 min. or until well blended. (Mixture will be thick.) Add 1 cup of the whipped topping; stir gently until well blended. Spread evenly onto bottom of crust. Top with 12 of the remaining wafers.

POUR remaining 1 cup milk into separate medium bowl. Add remaining dry pudding mix. Beat with wire whisk 2 min. Gently stir in 1 cup of the remaining whipped topping; spread evenly over wafer layer. Refrigerate at least 3 hours. Meanwhile, melt chocolate as directed on package. Dip one-third of each of the remaining 10 wafers in chocolate. Turn wafers slightly, then dip the opposite side of each wafer in chocolate, leaving a V-shaped portion of each wafer uncoated in the center. Use a wooden toothpick to decorate wafers with some of the remaining chocolate to resemble bow ties. Add "buttons" with small drops of the remaining chocolate. Place on wax paper-covered baking sheets; let stand until chocolate is firm.

TOP pie with remaining whipped topping just before serving. Garnish with decorated wafers. Store any leftover dessert in refrigerator.

Makes 10 servings, 1 slice each.

Nutrition Information Per Serving: 340 calories, 16g total fat, 10g saturated fat, 450mg sodium, 48g carbohydrate, 3g protein.

Jazz It Up:

Garnish with colored sprinkles just before serving.

HOLIDAY "EGGNOG" SQUARES

Prep: 15 min. ● Total: 3 hours 15 min. (incl. refrigerating)

67 NILLA Wafers, divided

¼ cup (½ stick) butter or margarine, divided

2 Tbsp. sugar

3 squares BAKER'S Premium White Baking Chocolate

2 cups cold milk

2 pkg. (4-serving size each) JELL-O Vanilla Flavor Instant Pudding & Pie Filling

¾ tsp. rum extract

¼ tsp. ground nutmeg

1½ cups thawed COOL WHIP Whipped Topping

CRUSH 35 of the wafers; place in medium bowl. Melt 3 Tbsp. of the butter. Add to wafer crumbs along with the sugar; mix well. Spoon into 9-inch square pan; press firmly onto bottom of pan. Set aside.

PLACE chocolate and remaining 1 Tbsp. butter in small microwaveable bowl. Microwave on HIGH 1 min. or until butter is melted. Stir until chocolate is completely melted and mixture is well blended. Drizzle over crust.

POUR milk into large bowl. Add dry pudding mixes, extract and nutmeg. Beat with wire whisk 2 min. Gently stir in whipped topping. Spread half of the pudding mixture over crust; top with 16 of the remaining wafers. Cover with remaining pudding mixture. Refrigerate at least 3 hours or until firm. Cut into squares just before serving. Garnish with the remaining 16 wafers. Store any leftover dessert in refrigerator.

Makes 16 servings, 1 square each.

Nutrition Information Per Serving (without cookie dipped in chocolate): 210 calories, 9g total fat, 5g saturated fat, 280mg sodium, 31g carbohydrate, 2g protein.

Jazz It Up:

Prepare dessert and refrigerate as directed. Meanwhile, partially dip the remaining 16 wafers in additional melted BAKER'S Premium White Baking Chocolate. Immediately sprinkle coated portions of wafers with sprinkles. Let stand until chocolate is firm. Store at room temperature until ready to use as directed.

NILLA TORTONI "CAKE"

Prep: 20 min. ● Total: 4 hours 20 min. (incl. freezing)

1 pkg. (12 oz.) **NILLA** Wafers, coarsely crushed, divided

1 cup **PLANTERS** Slivered Almonds, toasted, divided

1 container (1¾ qt.) vanilla ice cream, softened, divided

½ cup caramel topping

SPRINKLE 1 cup of the wafer crumbs and ⅓ cup of the almonds onto bottom of 9-inch springform pan; top with half of the ice cream. Repeat layers of the wafer crumbs, almonds and ice cream. Top with remaining wafer crumbs and almonds; press into ice cream with back of spoon to secure. Cover.

FREEZE at least 4 hours.

REMOVE side of pan before cutting dessert into wedges to serve. Drizzle with caramel topping. Store any leftover dessert in freezer.

Makes 16 servings, 1 wedge each.

Substitute: Prepare as directed, substituting your favorite flavor ice cream.

Nutrition Information Per Serving: 280 calories, 14g total fat, 5g saturated fat, 150mg sodium, 37g carbohydrate, 5g protein.

How to Toast Nuts:

Spread almonds into single layer in shallow baking pan. Bake at 350°F for 5 to 7 min. or until lightly toasted, stirring occasionally.

OREO CHOCOLATE CHEESECAKE

Prep: 30 min. ● Total: 6 hours 15 min. (incl. refrigerating)

38 **OREO** Chocolate Sandwich Cookies, divided

5 Tbsp. butter or margarine, melted

5 squares **BAKER'S** Semi-Sweet Baking Chocolate, divided

1 pkg. (8 oz.) **PHILADELPHIA** Cream Cheese, softened

½ cup sugar

1½ cups **BREAKSTONE'S** or **KNUDSEN** Sour Cream, divided

2 eggs

1 tsp. vanilla

2 Tbsp. sugar

PREHEAT oven to 325°F, if using a silver 9-inch springform pan (or to 300°F if using a dark nonstick 9-inch springform pan). Finely crush 24 of the cookies; mix with butter. Press firmly onto bottom of pan. Stand remaining 14 cookies around inside edge of pan, firmly pressing bottom edge of each cookie into crust. Set aside.

MELT 4 of the chocolate squares in small saucepan on low heat; set aside. Beat cream cheese and ½ cup sugar in large bowl with electric mixer on medium speed until well blended. Add ½ cup of the sour cream, the eggs and vanilla; beat until well blended. Add melted chocolate; mix well. Pour over crust.

BAKE 35 to 40 min. or until top of cheesecake is slightly puffed and center is almost set. Mix remaining 1 cup sour cream and the 2 Tbsp. sugar; spread over cheesecake. Bake an additional 5 min. Run knife or metal spatula around rim of pan to loosen cake; cool before removing rim.

MELT remaining chocolate square; drizzle over cheesecake. Refrigerate at least 4 hours. Garnish with fresh raspberries, chocolate curls and fresh mint just before serving, if desired. Store any leftover dessert in refrigerator.

Makes 14 servings, 1 slice each.

Nutrition Information Per Serving (without garnish): 380 calories, 25g total fat, 12g saturated fat, 300mg sodium, 37g carbohydrate, 5g protein.

How to Make Chocolate Curls:

Let additional square(s) of **BAKER'S** Semi-Sweet Baking Chocolate come to room temperature. Carefully draw a vegetable peeler at an angle across the chocolate square to make curls.

HOLIDAY BLACK FOREST PIE

Prep: 15 min. • Total: 3 hours 15 min. (incl. refrigerating)

34 **OREO** Chocolate Sandwich Cookies, divided

¼ cup (½ stick) butter or margarine, melted

2 cups cold milk

2 pkg. (4-serving size each) or 1 pkg. (8-serving size) **JELL-O** Chocolate Flavor Instant Pudding & Pie Filling

1 tub (8 oz.) **COOL WHIP** Whipped Topping, thawed, divided

1 cup cherry pie filling

1 square **BAKER'S** Semi-Sweet Baking Chocolate, melted

CUT 10 of the cookies into quarters; set aside for later use. Finely crush remaining 24 cookies; mix with the butter. Press firmly onto bottom and up side of 9-inch pie plate. Refrigerate while preparing filling.

POUR milk into large bowl. Add dry pudding mixes. Beat with wire whisk 2 min. or until well blended. (Mixture will be thick.) Spoon 1½ cups of the pudding into crust. Top with the reserved cookie pieces. Gently stir 1½ cups of the whipped topping into remaining pudding; spoon over pie.

REFRIGERATE 3 hours. Cover with remaining whipped topping just before serving. Top with the cherry pie filling. Drizzle with melted chocolate. Store any leftover dessert in refrigerator.

Makes 10 servings, 1 slice each.

Shortcut: Substitute 1 pkg. (6 oz.) **OREO** Pie Crust for the homemade crumb crust.

Nutrition Information Per Serving: 420 calories, 18g total fat, 11g saturated fat, 600mg sodium, 64g carbohydrate, 4g protein.

How to Make Mess-Free Cookie Crumbs:

Crushing cookies into crumbs can be a messy task. To keep the crumbs contained, place the whole cookies in a resealable plastic bag. Squeeze the air from the bag, and seal the bag. Run a rolling pin back and forth over the cookies until finely crushed.

LEMON-GINGER REFRIGERATOR ROLL

Prep: 20 min. • Total: 8 hours 20 min. (incl. refrigerating)

1 **cup cold fat free milk**

1 **pkg. (4-serving size) JELL-O Lemon Flavor Instant Pudding & Pie Filling**

1½ **cups thawed COOL WHIP LITE Whipped Topping**

30 **NABISCO Ginger Snaps**

POUR milk into medium bowl. Add dry pudding mix. Beat with wire whisk 2 min. or until well blended. Gently stir in whipped topping.

SPREAD about 1½ tsp. of the pudding mixture onto each cookie. Begin stacking cookies together, standing on edge on serving platter to make a log. Frost with remaining pudding mixture.

REFRIGERATE at least 8 hours or overnight. Cut diagonally into 12 slices to serve. Store any leftover dessert in refrigerator.

Makes 12 servings, 1 slice each.

Make Ahead: Be sure to refrigerate this dessert at least 8 hours before serving to allow the cookies to soften to the desired cake-like texture.

Nutrition Information Per Serving: 130 calories, 3g total fat, 1.5g saturated fat, 260mg sodium, 25g carbohydrate, 2g protein.

HONEY MAID GINGERBREAD HOLIDAY HOUSE

Prep: 1 hour ● Total: 1 hour

½ **cup powdered sugar**

1¼ **tsp. water**

9 squares **HONEY MAID** Gingerbread Grahams

18 squares **POST** Honey Nut Shredded Wheat Cereal

4 pieces **POST GRAPE-NUTS O'S**

2 Tbsp. **POST** Fruity **PEBBLES** Cereal

MIX sugar and water. Add small amount of additional water, if necessary, to make a very thick frosting; spoon into small resealable plastic bag. Cut small piece from one of the bottom corners of bag to use for piping frosting; set aside.

ASSEMBLE house, using 1 of the grahams for the floor and 4 of the remaining grahams for the walls, securing with frosting. Cut 1 of the remaining grahams diagonally in half; attach cut-sides of graham halves to opposite sides of house to form roof supports. Attach 2 of the remaining grahams with frosting to form roof, sealing all edges with frosting. Let stand until set.

CUT remaining graham to use for door and 2 windows; secure to house with frosting. Attach shredded wheat cereal to roof for shingles and **GRAPE-NUTS** to top of roof for chimney, using frosting to secure. Decorate with **PEBBLES** Cereal to resemble lights, wreath and walkway, attaching with frosting as needed.

Makes 1 house.

The FLINTSTONES and all related characters and elements are trademarks of © Hanna-Barbera.

Take-Along:

This decorative house makes a great gift to bring to a holiday party. Assemble house on a disposable decorative tray or platter; sprinkle BAKER'S ANGEL FLAKE Coconut on tray around house for snow. Stand a few TEDDY GRAHAMS Graham Snacks around house. Then wrap with a large sheet of clear or colored cellophane tied at the top with a festive ribbon.

GIFT-GIVING
FAVORITES

Great-tasting, innovative
gifts from your kitchen

EASY OREO TRUFFLES

Prep: 30 min. ● Total: 1 hour 30 min. (incl. refrigerating)

- 1 pkg. (1 lb. 2 oz.) **OREO** Chocolate Sandwich Cookies, finely crushed, divided
- 1 pkg. (8 oz.) **PHILADELPHIA** Cream Cheese, softened
- 2 pkg. (8 squares each) **BAKER'S** Semi-Sweet Baking Chocolate, melted

MIX 3 cups of the cookie crumbs and the cream cheese until well blended. Shape into 42 (1-inch) balls.

DIP balls in melted chocolate; place on wax paper-covered baking sheet. (Any leftover melted chocolate can be stored in tightly covered container at room temperature and saved for another use.) Sprinkle with remaining cookie crumbs.

REFRIGERATE 1 hour or until firm. Store any leftover truffles in tightly covered container in refrigerator.

Makes 3½ doz. or 42 servings, 1 truffle each.

Nutrition Information Per Serving: 100 calories, 6g total fat, 3g saturated fat, 85mg sodium, 12g carbohydrate, 1g protein.

Jazz It Up:

Sprinkle truffles with colored sugar or sprinkles in addition to or in place of the cookie crumbs.

OREO CANDY CANE BARK

Prep: 10 min ● Total: 4 hours 10 min (incl. refrigerating)

3 pkg. (6 oz. each) **BAKER'S** Premium White Baking Chocolate

15 **OREO** Chocolate Sandwich Cookies, coarsely chopped (about 2 cups)

3 candy canes, crushed (about ¼ cup)

COVER large baking sheet with foil; set aside. Microwave chocolate in large microwaveable bowl on HIGH 2 min. or until almost melted, stirring every 30 sec. Stir until chocolate is completely melted. Stir in chopped cookies.

SPREAD immediately onto prepared baking sheet. Sprinkle with crushed candy canes; press candy lightly into chocolate with back of spoon.

REFRIGERATE 4 hours or until firm. Break into pieces. Store in tightly covered container in refrigerator.

Makes 1½ lb. or 18 servings.

Substitute: Prepare as directed, substituting 10 starlight mint candies for the candy canes.

Make Ahead: Bark can be stored in refrigerator up to 2 weeks.

Nutrition Information Per Serving: 210 calories, 11 g total fat, 6g saturated fat, 70mg sodium, 27g carbohydrate, 2g protein.

How to Easily Crush Candy Canes:

Crushing candy canes can be a messy task. To keep the crushed candy contained, place candy canes in a resealable plastic bag and squeeze air from bag; seal. Use a rolling pin or meat mallet to crush the candy into small pieces.

GRAHAM BREAK-AWAYS

Prep: 10 min. ● Total: 25 min.

---

12 **HONEY MAID** Honey Grahams, broken in half (24 squares)

½ cup (1 stick) butter or margarine

¾ cup firmly packed brown sugar

1 cup **BAKER'S** Semi-Sweet Chocolate Chunks

½ cup finely chopped **PLANTERS** Pecans

PREHEAT oven to 350°F. Arrange graham squares in single layer in 15 × 10 × 1-inch baking pan.

PLACE butter and sugar in medium saucepan. Bring to boil on medium heat; cook 2 min. Pour over grahams; immediately spread to completely cover all grahams.

BAKE 6 to 8 min. or until sugar mixture is lightly browned and bubbly. Sprinkle with chocolate chunks. Bake an additional 1 to 2 min. or until chocolate is melted. Remove from oven; immediately spread chocolate over grahams. Sprinkle with pecans; press lightly into chocolate with back of spoon. Cool completely. Break into 24 squares; break squares in half to form rectangles.

Makes 24 servings, 2 pieces each.

Substitute: Substitute **PLANTERS** Cocktail Peanuts for the pecans.

Nutrition Information Per Serving: 140 calories, 8g total fat, 4g saturated fat, 90mg sodium, 17g carbohydrate, 1g protein.

Gift Giving:

Save cookie tins of all shapes and sizes throughout the year. Or buy inexpensive jars, baking pans, mugs or festive serving dishes for packaging your edible gifts. The packaging then becomes a gift too!

HONEY MAID "GINGERBREAD"

Prep: 10 min. ● Total: 1 hour 10 min. (incl. cooling)

18 **HONEY MAID** Gingerbread Grahams, finely crushed (about 2¼ cups)

¼ cup flour

¼ cup granulated sugar

2 tsp. **CALUMET** Baking Powder

¼ tsp. baking soda

1 cup fat free milk

1 egg, lightly beaten

2 Tbsp. honey

2 to 3 tsp. water, divided

½ cup powdered sugar

PREHEAT oven to 350°F. Mix graham crumbs, flour, granulated sugar, baking powder and baking soda in medium bowl. Add milk, egg and honey; stir just until blended. Spoon into 3 lightly greased 5½×3¼×2-inch disposable mini loaf pans.

BAKE 30 min. or until wooden toothpick inserted into centers comes out clean. Cool completely.

ADD 2 tsp. of the water to powdered sugar; stir until well blended. Add remaining 1 tsp. water if necessary until glaze is of desired consistency. Drizzle over cooled loaves. Let stand until glaze is firm.

Makes 12 servings or 3 loaves, 4 servings each.

Nutrition Information Per Serving (with glaze): 170 calories, 2.5g total fat, 0.5g saturated fat, 280mg sodium, 34g carbohydrate, 3g protein.

Jazz It Up:

This "gingerbread" makes a great gift to bring to a holiday party. Cool completely and wrap in plastic wrap before placing in a holiday-themed basket or container.

LEMON-COCONUT SQUARES

Prep: 10 min. ● Total: 3 hours 40 min. (incl. refrigerating)

35 NILLA Wafers, finely crushed (about 1⅓ cups)

1 cup sugar, divided

¼ cup (½ stick) butter or margarine, melted

1 tsp. grated lemon peel

2 eggs

¼ cup lemon juice

2 Tbsp. flour

½ tsp. CALUMET Baking Powder

¼ tsp. salt

⅓ cup BAKER'S ANGEL FLAKE Coconut

PREHEAT oven to 350°F. Mix wafer crumbs, ¼ cup of the sugar, the butter and lemon peel until well blended. Press firmly into 8-inch square baking pan. Bake 8 min.

BEAT eggs and remaining ¾ cup sugar in small bowl with wire whisk until thickened and well blended. Add lemon juice, flour, baking powder and salt; mix well. Pour over crust; sprinkle with coconut.

BAKE 25 to 30 min. or until center is set and top is lightly browned. Cool completely. Cover and refrigerate several hours or until chilled before cutting to serve. Store in tightly covered container in refrigerator.

Makes 20 servings, 1 square each.

Nutrition Information Per Serving: 110 calories, 4.5g total fat, 2g saturated fat, 95mg sodium, 16g carbohydrate, 1g protein.

PLANTERS DOUBLE FANTASY FUDGE

Prep: 30 min. • Total: 4 hours 30 min. (incl. cooling)

6 cups sugar, divided

1½ cups (3 sticks) butter or margarine, divided

2 small cans (5 oz. each) evaporated milk (about ⅔ cup each)

1 cup peanut butter

2 jars (7 oz. each) **JET-PUFFED** Marshmallow Creme, divided

2 cups chopped **PLANTERS** Dry Roasted Peanuts, divided

2 tsp. vanilla, divided

1½ pkg. (12 squares) **BAKER'S** Semi-Sweet Baking Chocolate

LINE 13×9-inch pan with foil, with ends of foil extending over sides of pan. Place 3 cups of the sugar, ¾ cup (1½ sticks) of the butter and 1 can of the evaporated milk in heavy 3-qt. saucepan. Bring to full rolling boil on medium heat, stirring constantly. Boil 4 min. or until candy thermometer reaches 234°F, stirring constantly to prevent scorching. Remove from heat.

ADD peanut butter and contents of 1 of the marshmallow creme jars; stir until completely melted. Add 1 cup of the peanuts and 1 tsp. of the vanilla; mix well. Pour immediately into prepared pan; spread to evenly cover bottom of pan. Set aside.

PLACE remaining 3 cups sugar, the remaining ¾ cup (1½ sticks) butter and the remaining can of evaporated milk in large heavy saucepan. Bring to full rolling boil on medium heat, stirring constantly. Boil 4 min. or until candy thermometer reaches 234°F, stirring constantly to prevent scorching. Remove from heat.

ADD chocolate and remaining jar of marshmallow creme; stir until completely melted. Add ½ cup of the remaining peanuts and the remaining 1 tsp. vanilla; mix well. Pour immediately over peanut butter fudge layer in pan. Spread to evenly cover peanut butter fudge; sprinkle with remaining ½ cup peanuts. Cool at room temperature at least 4 hours before cutting into small pieces to serve. Store in tightly covered container at room temperature.

Makes 6 lb. or 70 servings, 1 piece each.

Important Note: If you are only able to purchase a large (12 oz.) can of evaporated milk, be sure to use only ⅔ cup for each fudge layer so that the fudge will set.

High Altitude: For every 1,000 feet above sea level, decrease final recommended cooking temperature by 2°F.

Nutrition Information Per Serving: 190 calories, 10g total fat, 3.5g saturated fat, 70mg sodium, 26g carbohydrate, 3g protein.

Cooking Know-How:

If you don't have a candy thermometer, bring sugar mixture to full rolling boil on medium heat, then begin timing 4 min. while mixture continues to boil, stirring constantly.

OREO HOLIDAY TREATS

Prep: 30 min. • Total: 30 min.

8 **OREO** Pure Milk Chocolate Covered Sandwich Cookies or **OREO** White Fudge Covered Chocolate Sandwich Cookies

Suggested decorations: decorating icings, holiday sprinkles, colored sugars

DRAW stars, trees, holiday ornaments or wreaths on tops of cookies with icing. Decorate with sprinkles or colored sugar, if desired.

Makes 8 servings, 1 cookie each.

Gift-Giving:

These decorative cookies make a great gift. Remove outer wrapping and plastic tray from original cookie box; line box with parchment paper. Place decorated cookies in mini holiday paper cupcake liners before placing in box. Wrap with colorful plastic wrap and festive ribbon, attaching a candy cane or small holiday ornament to top of package with the ribbon.

Cheese Casseroles
& MORE

Presented By:

Contents

I have to confess that autumn is my favorite time of year. Whether it's the cool evenings, the colorful parade of leaves, or the fall produce in our local markets, autumn has always signaled the start of something cozy.

Another one of my favorite things about this time of year is the return of comfort food. Enjoy the start of autumn with some of your favorite Kraft Kitchens dishes using **KRAFT Grated Parmesan, PHILADELPHIA, and Natural Shredded Cheeses**. You'll find inspiring recipes to help balance your busy schedule with the demands of taste, convenience, and health—all without putting a strain on the family finances! These simple recipes will let you spend your time with your family, instead of in the kitchen.

We've included recipes for all occasions—from casual get-togethers and weeknight suppers, to easy, make-ahead casseroles and delicious side dishes that will quickly become part of your "go-to" recipe collection. You'll be able to recreate your family's restaurant favorites, include a serving of fresh and tasty vegetable dishes, and serve up classic and mouth-watering one-pan dishes.

You'll love the way a quick sprinkle of **KRAFT Parmesan** instantly adds a burst of flavor to so many of your dishes! **PHILADELPHIA Cream Cheese** adds that distinctive rich and creamy taste to any meal. And who could pass up a dish with the ooey, gooey goodness of **KRAFT Natural Shredded Cheese**?

There's no better way to celebrate autumn than by reconnecting with your family around the kitchen table with a home-cooked, soul-satisfying casserole that will have everyone asking for more. And just remember—only you will know how quick and easy it actually was!

Carrie Conway, *Kraft Kitchens*

Chicken-Parmesan Bundles
(page 264)

DIPS &

APPETIZERS

BLT Dip

PREP: 15 min. **TOTAL:** 15 min.

- 1 pkg. (8 oz.) **PHILADELPHIA** Cream Cheese, softened
- ¾ cup shredded or chopped romaine lettuce
- 2 plum tomatoes, seeded, chopped
- 4 slices **OSCAR MAYER** Bacon, crisply cooked, drained and crumbled

SPREAD cream cheese onto bottom of 9-inch pie plate.

TOP with lettuce and tomatoes; sprinkle with bacon.

SERVE with **WHEAT THINS** Snack Crackers or assorted cut-up fresh vegetables.

Makes 2 cups or 16 servings, 2 Tbsp. each.

Make Ahead: Dip can be stored, tightly covered, in refrigerator up to 1 hour before serving.

How to Soften Cream Cheese: Place completely unwrapped package of cream cheese in microwaveable 9-inch pie plate. Microwave on HIGH 15 sec. or just until softened. Spread onto bottom of pie plate, then continue as directed.

Cheesy Spinach and Artichoke Dip

PREP: 10 min. **TOTAL:** 30 min.

- 1 can (14 oz.) artichoke hearts, drained, finely chopped
- 1 pkg. (10 oz.) frozen chopped spinach, thawed, drained
- ¾ cup **KRAFT** Grated Parmesan Cheese
- ¾ cup **KRAFT** Light Mayonnaise
- ½ cup **KRAFT** 2% Milk Shredded Mozzarella Cheese
- ½ tsp. garlic powder

HEAT oven to 350°F. Mix all ingredients; spoon into quiche dish or pie plate.

BAKE 20 min. or until heated through.

SERVE with **TRISCUIT** Reduced Fat Crackers and assorted cut-up fresh vegetables.

Makes 2¾ cups or 22 servings, 2 Tbsp. each.

Awesome Spinach and Mushroom Dip: Substitute 1 cup chopped fresh mushrooms for the artichokes.

Layered Italian Dip

PREP: 10 min. **TOTAL:** 25 min.

1 **pkg. (8 oz.) PHILADELPHIA Cream Cheese, softened**

¼ **cup KRAFT Grated Parmesan Cheese**

⅓ **cup pesto**

½ **cup roasted red peppers, drained, chopped**

1 **cup KRAFT Shredded Mozzarella Cheese**

HEAT oven to 350°F. Mix cream cheese and Parmesan cheese; spread into pie plate.

TOP with remaining ingredients.

BAKE 15 min. or until heated through. Serve with **NABISCO** Crackers.

Makes 2 cups or 16 servings, 2 Tbsp. each.

Variation: Prepare using **PHILADELPHIA** Neufchâtel Cheese, and **KRAFT** 2% Milk Shredded Mozzarella Cheese.

Special Extra: Garnish with sliced black olives and fresh basil.

Hot Crab Dip

PREP: 15 min. **TOTAL:** 45 min.

- 2 pkg. (8 oz. each) **PHILADELPHIA** Cream Cheese, softened
- 2 cans (6 oz. each) crabmeat, drained, flaked
- ½ cup **KRAFT** Shredded Parmesan Cheese
- 2 green onions, sliced
- 2 Tbsp. dry white wine
- 1 Tbsp. **KRAFT** Horseradish Sauce
- 1 tsp. hot pepper sauce

HEAT oven to 350°F. Beat all ingredients with mixer until blended.

SPOON into pie plate.

BAKE 25 to 30 min. or until lightly browned. Serve with **NABISCO** Crackers and cut up fresh vegetables.

Makes 3 ½ cups or 28 servings, 2 Tbsp. each.

Keeping It Safe: Even canned crabmeat can contain tiny pieces of shell, so use your just-washed fingers to pick over the crabmeat before adding to a recipe.

Substitute: Prepare using **PHILADELPHIA** Neufchâtel Cheese.

Bacon Appetizer Crescents

PREP: 30 min. **TOTAL:** 45 min.

- 1 pkg. (8 oz.) **PHILADELPHIA** Cream Cheese, softened
- 8 slices **OSCAR MAYER** Bacon, crisply cooked, crumbled
- ⅓ cup **KRAFT** Grated Parmesan Cheese
- ¼ cup finely chopped onions
- 2 Tbsp. chopped fresh parsley
- 1 Tbsp. milk
- 2 cans (8 oz. each) refrigerated crescent dinner rolls

HEAT oven to 375°F. Mix all ingredients except dough.

SEPARATE each can of dough into 4 rectangles; firmly press perforations together to seal. Spread each rectangle with ¼ of cream cheese mixture. Cut each rectangle into 12 wedges; roll up, starting at short ends. Place, seam-sides down, on greased baking sheet.

BAKE 12 to 15 min. or until golden brown.

Makes 8 doz. or 24 servings, 4 crescents each.

Substitute: Prepare using **PHILADELPHIA** Neufchâtel Cheese.

Special Extra: Sprinkle lightly with poppy seeds before baking.

KRAFT Parmesan Breadsticks

PREP: 15 min. **TOTAL:** 30 min.

1 **can (11 oz.) refrigerated soft breadsticks, separated**

3 **Tbsp. butter or margarine, melted**

½ **cup KRAFT Grated Parmesan Cheese**

HEAT oven to 350°F. Dip breadsticks in butter; coat lightly with cheese.

TWIST breadsticks; place on baking sheet.

BAKE 13 to 15 min. or until golden brown.

Makes 12 servings, 1 breadstick each.

Serving Suggestion: These breadsticks are a good accompaniment to a serving of grilled meat and a crisp mixed green salad.

Shapes & Sizes: Prepare as directed, shaping twisted breadstick halves into letters, numbers, pretzel shapes or tying into knots before dipping in butter and coating with cheese.

KRAFT Parmesan Bruschetta

PREP: 15 min. **TOTAL:** 19 min.

  1 **large tomato, chopped**

  ½ **cup KRAFT Grated Parmesan Cheese**

  2 **cloves garlic, minced**

  ⅓ **cup olive oil, divided**

  ¼ **cup sliced fresh basil leaves**

  1 **loaf French bread (1 lb.), cut into 18 slices**

HEAT broiler. Combine tomatoes, cheese, garlic, 2 Tbsp. oil and basil.

BRUSH remaining oil onto both sides of bread slices.

BROIL, 6 inches from heat, 2 min. on each side or until golden brown. Top with tomato mixture.

Makes 18 servings, 1 appetizer each.

Substitute: Substitute 1 tsp. dried basil leaves for the fresh basil leaves.

Substitute: Prepare using **KRAFT** Shredded Parmesan Cheese; or **KRAFT** Shredded Parmesan, Romano and Asiago Cheese.

Spinach-Stuffed Mushrooms

PREP: 15 min. **TOTAL:** 35 min.

- 1 pkg. (6 oz.) **STOVE TOP** Stuffing Mix for Chicken
- 1½ cups hot water
- 40 fresh mushrooms (2 lb.)
- 2 Tbsp. butter
- 2 cloves garlic, minced
- 1 pkg. (10 oz.) frozen chopped spinach, thawed, well drained
- 1 cup **KRAFT** Shredded Low-Moisture Part-Skim Mozzarella Cheese
- 1 cup **KRAFT** Grated Parmesan Cheese

HEAT oven to 400°F. Mix stuffing mix and hot water. Remove stems from mushrooms; chop stems. Melt butter in skillet on medium heat. Add chopped stems and garlic; cook and stir until tender. Stir into prepared stuffing along with spinach and cheeses.

SPOON into mushrooms; place in shallow baking pan.

BAKE 20 min. or until filling is heated through.

Makes 40 servings, 1 mushroom each.

Leftover Stuffing: Since mushrooms vary in size, you may have some leftover stuffing mixture. If so, heat it and serve as a side dish with chicken.

SIDE DISHES

KRAFT Golden Parmesan Potatoes

PREP: 10 min. **TOTAL:** 55 min.

- 2 lb. new potatoes, quartered
- ¼ cup olive oil
- 1½ tsp. Italian seasoning
- 2 cloves garlic, minced
- ⅓ cup **KRAFT** Grated Parmesan Cheese

HEAT oven to 400°F. Toss potatoes with oil, seasoning and garlic. Add cheese; mix lightly.

SPREAD into 15×10×1-inch baking pan.

BAKE 45 min. or until potatoes are tender.

Makes 6 servings.

Substitute: Prepare using **KRAFT** Grated Parmesan and Romano Cheese.

Zesty Grilled Veggies

PREP: 10 min. **TOTAL:** 20 min.

4 **zucchini (1½ lb.), cut diagonally into ½-inch-thick slices**

3 **each: red and yellow bell peppers (1¾ lb.), cut into ½-inch-wide strips**

¼ **cup KRAFT Zesty Italian Dressing**

¼ **cup KRAFT Grated Parmesan Cheese**

HEAT grill to medium. Place vegetables in grill basket.

GRILL 10 min. or until crisp-tender, turning occasionally. Place in large bowl.

ADD dressing; toss to coat. Sprinkle with cheese.

Makes 8 servings.

Cooking Know-How: Don't have a grill basket? Cover grill grate with large sheet of heavy-duty foil before heating as directed. Spread vegetables onto foil. Grill as directed, stirring occasionally.

How to Buy Peppers: Look for peppers with very bright colors and a firm thick flesh. Refrigerate unwashed peppers in a plastic bag for up to 2 weeks.

Cheesy Smashed Potatoes

PREP: 15 min. **TOTAL:** 35 min.

- 1 lb. red potatoes (about 3 small), cut into chunks
- 1 cup bite-size cauliflower florets
- ¼ cup **BREAKSTONE'S** Reduced Fat or **KNUDSEN** Light Sour Cream
- 1 cup **KRAFT** 2% Milk Shredded Sharp Cheddar Cheese

COOK vegetables in boiling water 20 min. or until tender. Drain; return to pan.

ADD sour cream; mash until light and fluffy. Stir in cheese.

Makes 6 servings, ½ cup each.

Substitute: Substitute 1 cup frozen cauliflower florets for the fresh cauliflower.

Use Your Microwave: Place potatoes and cauliflower in large microwaveable bowl; add water to cover. Cover with waxed paper. Microwave on HIGH 20 min. or until vegetables are very tender. Continue as directed.

Mashed Potato Layer Bake

PREP: 25 min. **TOTAL:** 45 min.

- 4 large white potatoes, peeled, chopped and cooked
- 2 large sweet potatoes, peeled, chopped and cooked
- 1 tub (8 oz.) **PHILADELPHIA** Chive & Onion Cream Cheese Spread, divided
- ½ cup **BREAKSTONE'S** or **KNUDSEN** Sour Cream, divided
- ¼ tsp. each: salt and black pepper
- ¼ cup **KRAFT** Shredded Parmesan Cheese, divided
- ¼ cup **KRAFT** Shredded Cheddar Cheese, divided

HEAT oven to 375°F. Place potatoes in separate bowls. Add ½ each of the cream cheese spread and sour cream to each bowl; season with salt and pepper. Mash until creamy.

STIR ½ the Parmesan cheese into white potatoes. Stir half of the Cheddar cheese into sweet potatoes. Alternately layer ½ each of the white potato and sweet potato mixtures in 2-qt. casserole dish. Repeat layers.

BAKE 15 min. Sprinkle with remaining cheeses; bake 5 min. or until melted.

Makes 14 servings, ½ cup each.

Make Ahead: Assemble casserole as directed but do not add the cheese topping. Refrigerate casserole and cheese topping separately up to 3 days. When ready to serve, bake casserole as directed, increasing baking time as needed until casserole is heated through. Top with remaining cheeses and continue as directed.

Easy "Baked" Tomatoes

PREP: 5 min. **TOTAL:** 20 min.

- 4 **tomatoes, cut in half**
- ¼ cup **KRAFT** Balsamic Vinaigrette Dressing
- ¼ cup **KRAFT** Grated Parmesan Cheese

HEAT grill to medium. Place tomatoes, cut-sides up, in disposable foil pan. Top with dressing and cheese. Place pan on grate of grill; close lid.

GRILL 15 min. or until tomatoes are soft and cheese is lightly browned.

Makes 4 servings.

How to Use Your Oven: Heat oven to 350°F. Place tomato halves, cut-sides up, in a 13×9-inch baking dish. Top with dressing and cheese as directed. Bake 15 to 20 min. or until tomatoes are soft and cheese is lightly browned.

Special Extra: Sprinkle with 1 Tbsp. chopped fresh basil or parsley before grilling as directed.

Substitute: For variety, prepare with **KRAFT** Sun-Dried Tomato Dressing.

Cheesy Harvest Vegetables

PREP: 35 min. **TOTAL:** 1 hour 5 min.

2 **lb. mixed fall vegetables (butternut squash, sweet potatoes, turnips, parsnips and carrots), peeled, cut into 1-inch cubes**

3 **cups milk**

1 **pkg. (8 oz.) PHILADELPHIA Cream Cheese, cubed**

1 **cup KRAFT Shredded Parmesan Cheese**

⅛ **tsp. ground nutmeg**

8 **RITZ Crackers, crushed**

HEAT oven to 350°F. Bring vegetables and milk to boil in large saucepan on medium-high heat. Reduce heat to medium-low; simmer 20 min. or until vegetables are tender, stirring occasionally. Add cream cheese; cook until melted, stirring frequently. Stir in Parmesan cheese and nutmeg.

SPOON into greased 2-qt. casserole dish; sprinkle with crumbs.

BAKE 30 min. or until heated through.

Makes 10 servings, about ¾ cup each.

Size-Wise: Enjoy a serving of this cheesy vegetable side dish at your next special occasion.

Make Ahead: Assemble recipe as directed except do not add crumb topping. Refrigerate up to 24 hours. When ready to serve, sprinkle with the cracker crumbs. Bake as directed, increasing the baking time to 40 min. or until heated through.

Easy Vegetable Toss

PREP: 15 min. **TOTAL:** 3 hours 15 min. (incl. refrigerating)

- **1 lb. broccoli florets**
- **1 lb. cauliflower florets**
- **½ lb. green beans**
- **1 large red bell pepper, cut into strips**
- **½ cup KRAFT Zesty Italian Dressing**
- **⅓ cup KRAFT Shredded Parmesan Cheese**

COOK broccoli, cauliflower and beans in boiling water 3 to 5 min. or just until crisp-tender. (Do not overcook.) Drain. Immediately rinse with very cold water; drain again. Place in large bowl.

STIR in peppers. Refrigerate several hours or until chilled.

ADD dressing and cheese just before serving; mix lightly.

Makes 16 servings, ¾ cup each.

Serve it Hot: For a change of pace, serve hot. Cook vegetables as directed; drain. Add remaining ingredients; mix lightly. Serve immediately.

Variation: Prepare as directed, using **KRAFT** Sun-Dried Tomato Dressing and **KRAFT** Grated Parmesan Cheese.

Parmesan Zucchini

PREP: 10 min. **TOTAL:** 40 min.

4 zucchini (1 lb.), thinly sliced

½ lb. mushrooms, thinly sliced

1 cup spaghetti sauce

1 cup **KRAFT** Shredded Low-Moisture Part-Skim Mozzarella Cheese

⅓ cup **KRAFT** Grated Parmesan Cheese

HEAT oven to 400°F. Combine vegetables and sauce; spoon into 13×9-inch baking dish sprayed with cooking spray.

BAKE 25 min. or until zucchini is tender. Sprinkle with cheeses; bake 5 min. or until melted.

Makes 6 servings.

Creative Leftovers: Refrigerate any leftovers. To reheat, sprinkle with desired amount of additional mozzarella and/or Parmesan cheese; cover. Bake at 350°F for 20 min. or until heated through.

Substitute: Prepare using **KRAFT** Grate-It-Fresh Natural Parmesan Cheese.

Sautéed Spinach with Mushrooms

PREP: 10 min. **TOTAL:** 18 min.

- 2 **Tbsp. olive oil**
- 1 **pkg. (8 oz.) sliced fresh mushrooms**
- 2 **cloves garlic, minced**
- 2 **lb. fresh spinach leaves, cleaned, torn**
- ¼ **tsp. salt**
- ¼ **tsp. black pepper**
- ⅓ **cup KRAFT Grated Parmesan Cheese**

HEAT oil in large skillet on medium-high heat. Add mushrooms and garlic; cook and stir 5 min. or until mushrooms are tender. Reduce heat to medium.

ADD spinach, salt and pepper; cook and stir 3 min. or just until spinach is wilted.

SPRINKLE with cheese.

Makes 8 servings, ½ cup each.

Cooking Know-How: Spinach can be added in batches if your skillet does not accommodate all of the spinach at once. As soon as the spinach begins to wilt, add the remaining spinach.

Variation: Substitute 4 pkg. (10 oz. each) frozen spinach leaves, thawed and well drained, for the fresh spinach. Cook mushrooms and garlic as directed. Add spinach; cook until heated through, stirring frequently. Continue as directed.

CASSEROLES

Creamy Chicken and Pasta Casserole

PREP: 15 min. **TOTAL:** 40 min.

- ¾ cup each: chopped celery, red onions and red peppers
- 1 pkg. (8 oz.) **PHILADELPHIA** Cream Cheese, cubed
- 2 cups milk
- ¼ tsp. garlic salt
- 4 cups cooked rotini pasta
- 3 cups chopped cooked chicken breasts
- ½ cup **KRAFT** Grated Parmesan Cheese, divided

HEAT oven to 350°F. Heat large nonstick skillet sprayed with cooking spray on medium heat. Add vegetables; cook and stir 3 min. or until crisp-tender. Add cream cheese, milk and garlic salt; cook on low heat 3 to 5 min. or until cream cheese is melted, stirring frequently.

ADD pasta, chicken and ¼ cup Parmesan cheese; spoon into 2½-qt. casserole dish.

BAKE 20 to 25 min. or until heated through. Sprinkle with remaining Parmesan cheese.

Makes 6 servings.

Serving Suggestion: Serve with a mixed green salad tossed with your favorite **KRAFT** Dressing.

Variation: Prepare using **PHILADELPHIA** Neufchâtel Cheese, fat-free milk and whole wheat rotini pasta.

Easy Baked Manicotti

PREP: 25 min. **TOTAL:** 1 hour 5 min.

- 2 cups spaghetti sauce, divided
- 1 egg, beaten
- 1¾ cups **POLLY-O** Original Ricotta Cheese
- 1½ cups **KRAFT** Shredded Mozzarella Cheese
- ½ cup **KRAFT** Grated Parmesan Cheese
- ¼ cup pesto
- 12 manicotti shells, cooked, rinsed in cold water

HEAT oven to 350°F. Spread ¾ cup sauce onto bottom of 13×9-inch baking dish. Mix egg, cheeses and pesto; spoon into resealable plastic bag. Cut small hole in bottom corner of bag; use to squeeze cheese mixture into both ends of each shell.

PLACE in dish; top with remaining spaghetti sauce. Cover with foil.

BAKE 40 min. or until heated through.

Makes 6 servings, 2 manicotti each.

Size-Wise: Enjoy your favorite foods on occasion, but keep portion size in mind. This recipe makes enough to serve 6.

Make Ahead: Cook manicotti shells up to 1 day ahead. Place on greased tray, cover with plastic wrap and refrigerate until ready to fill.

Substitute: Substitute **BREAKSTONE'S** or **KNUDSEN** Cottage Cheese for the ricotta cheese and/or **KRAFT** Grated Romano Cheese for the Parmesan cheese.

One-Pan Chicken and Potato Bake

PREP: 10 min. **TOTAL:** 1 hour 10 min.

  4 bone-in chicken pieces (1½ lb.)

1½ lb. potatoes (about 3), cut into thin wedges

  ¼ cup KRAFT Zesty Italian Dressing

  ¼ cup KRAFT Grated Parmesan Cheese

  1 tsp. Italian seasoning

HEAT oven to 400°F. Place chicken and potatoes in 13×9-inch baking dish.

TOP with dressing, cheese and seasoning; cover with foil.

BAKE 1 hour or until chicken is cooked through (165°F), removing foil after 30 min.

Makes 4 servings.

Serving Suggestion: Serve a tossed green salad tossed with your favorite **KRAFT** Dressing.

Storage Tips for Potatoes: The best way to store potatoes is in a ventilated container in a dry dark place. Avoid storing potatoes with onions since the potatoes readily absorb odors.

New-Look Scalloped Potatoes and Ham

PREP: 30 min. **TOTAL:** 1 hour

- 4½ **lb. red potatoes, cut into ¼-inch-thick slices**
- 1 **container (16 oz.) BREAKSTONE'S FREE or KNUDSEN FREE Fat Free Sour Cream**
- ¾ **lb. (12 oz.) VELVEETA 2% Milk Pasteurized Prepared Cheese Product, cut into ½-inch cubes**
- ½ **lb. (½ of 1-lb. pkg.) OSCAR MAYER Smoked Ham, chopped**
- 4 **green onions, sliced**
- ¼ **cup KRAFT Grated Parmesan Cheese**

HEAT oven to 350°F. Cook potatoes in boiling water in covered large saucepan 10 to 12 min. or just until potatoes are tender; drain. Place ¾ of potatoes in large bowl. Add sour cream; mash until smooth. Stir in **VELVEETA**, ham and onions. Add remaining potatoes; mix lightly.

SPOON into 13×9-inch baking dish sprayed with cooking spray; sprinkle with Parmesan cheese.

BAKE 30 min. or until heated through.

Makes 16 servings, about 1 cup each.

Purchasing Potatoes: Look for firm, smooth, well-shaped potatoes that are free of wrinkles, cracks and blemishes. Avoid any with green-tinged skins or sprouting "eyes" or buds.

Size-Wise: Enjoy your favorite foods on occasion, but keep portion size in mind.

Easy Italian Pasta Bake

PREP: 20 min. **TOTAL:** 40 min.

- **1 lb. extra lean ground beef**
- **3 cups whole wheat penne pasta, cooked, drained**
- **1 jar (26 oz.) spaghetti sauce**
- **⅓ cup KRAFT Grated Parmesan Cheese, divided**
- **1½ cups KRAFT 2% Milk Shredded Mozzarella Cheese**

HEAT oven to 375°F. Brown meat in large skillet; drain. Stir in pasta, sauce and ½ the Parmesan cheese.

SPOON into 13×9-inch baking dish; top with remaining cheeses.

BAKE 20 min. or until heated through.

Makes 6 servings, 1⅓ cups each.

Substitute: Substitute regular penne pasta for the whole wheat penne pasta.

Special Extra: Brown meat with 1 tsp. Italian seasoning and 3 cloves garlic, minced.

Serving Suggestion: Serve with mixed green salad tossed with your favorite **KRAFT** Dressing.

Bruschetta Chicken Bake

PREP: 10 min. **TOTAL:** 40 min.

- 1 **can (14½ oz.) diced tomatoes, undrained**
- 1 **pkg. (6 oz.) STOVE TOP Stuffing Mix for Chicken**
- ½ **cup water**
- 2 **cloves garlic, minced**
- 1½ **lb. boneless, skinless chicken breasts, cut into bite-size pieces**
- 1 **tsp. dried basil leaves**
- 1 **cup KRAFT Shredded Low-Moisture Part-Skim Mozzarella Cheese**

HEAT oven to 400°F. Stir tomatoes, stuffing mix, water and garlic just until stuffing mix is moistened.

PLACE chicken in 13×9-inch baking dish; sprinkle with basil. Top with cheese and stuffing mixture.

BAKE 30 min. or until chicken is cooked through.

Makes 6 servings, 1 cup each.

Serving Suggestion: Serve with cooked green beans and a bagged green salad tossed with your favorite **KRAFT** Light Dressing.

Turkey-Parmesan Casserole

PREP: 20 min. **TOTAL:** 50 min.

- 8 oz. spaghetti, broken in half, uncooked
- 1 can (10¾ oz.) condensed cream of mushroom soup
- ¾ cup **BREAKSTONE'S** or **KNUDSEN** Sour Cream
- ¼ cup milk
- ⅓ cup **KRAFT** Grated Parmesan Cheese
- ¼ tsp. black pepper
- 3 cups frozen broccoli florets, thawed
- 2 cups chopped cooked turkey

HEAT oven to 350°F. Cook spaghetti as directed on package; drain.

MIX soup, sour cream, milk, Parmesan cheese and pepper in large bowl. Add spaghetti, broccoli and turkey; mix lightly. Spoon into 2-qt. casserole dish.

BAKE 25 to 30 min. or until heated through.

Makes: 6 servings, 1⅓ cups each.

Substitute: Substitute frozen cut green beans or peas for broccoli.

Substitute: Prepare using **KRAFT** Grated Parmesan and Romano Cheese.

Taco Bake

PREP: 15 min. **TOTAL:** 35 min.

- 1 pkg. (14 oz.) **KRAFT** Deluxe Macaroni & Cheese Dinner
- 1 lb. ground beef
- 1 pkg. **TACO BELL® HOME ORIGINALS®** Taco Seasoning Mix
- ¾ cup **BREAKSTONE'S** or **KNUDSEN** Sour Cream
- 1½ cups **KRAFT** Shredded Cheddar Cheese
- 1 cup **TACO BELL® HOME ORIGINALS®** Thick 'N Chunky Salsa

HEAT oven to 400°F. Prepare Dinner as directed on package. While Macaroni is cooking, cook meat with taco seasoning mix as directed on package.

STIR sour cream into prepared Dinner; spoon ½ into 8-inch square baking dish. Top with layers of meat mixture, 1 cup Cheddar cheese and remaining Dinner mixture; cover with foil.

BAKE 15 min. Top with salsa and remaining Cheddar. Bake, uncovered, 5 min. or until Cheddar is melted.

Makes 6 servings, 1 cup each.

Variation: Prepare using **BREAKSTONE'S** Reduced Fat or **KNUDSEN** Light Sour Cream, and **KRAFT** 2% Milk Shredded Cheddar Cheese.

Serving Suggestion: Serve with your favorite hot cooked vegetable, such as broccoli.

TACO BELL® and HOME ORIGINALS® are trademarks owned and licensed by Taco Bell Corp.

Cheesy Tuna Noodle Casserole

PREP: 20 min. **TOTAL:** 59 min.

- 1 **bag (16 oz.) frozen vegetable blend (broccoli, carrots, cauliflower)**
- 1 **pkg. (14 oz.) KRAFT Deluxe Macaroni & Cheese Dinner Made With 2% Milk Cheese**
- ¾ **cup fat-free milk**
- ¼ **cup KRAFT Light Zesty Italian Dressing**
- 1 **can (12 oz.) white tuna in water, drained, flaked**
- 1 **cup KRAFT 2% Milk Shredded Sharp Cheddar Cheese, divided**

HEAT oven to 375°F. Place vegetables in colander in sink. Cook Macaroni as directed on package. Pour over vegetables in colander to drain macaroni and quickly thaw vegetables.

RETURN macaroni and vegetables to saucepan. Stir in Cheese Sauce, milk and dressing. Add tuna and ½ cup Cheddar cheese; mix well. Spoon into 2-qt. casserole dish; cover with foil.

BAKE 35 min. or until heated through. Uncover; top with remaining Cheddar cheese. Bake 3 to 4 min. or until cheese is melted.

Makes 5 servings, about 1½ cups each.

Substitute: Substitute 1 lb. extra lean ground beef, cooked and drained, for the tuna.

Make Ahead: Assemble casserole as directed; cover. Refrigerate up to 24 hours. When ready to serve, bake, covered, at 375°F for 40 to 45 min. or until heated through. Remove from oven; uncover. Sprinkle with remaining Cheddar cheese. Let stand 5 min. or until cheese is melted.

Layered Enchilada Bake

PREP: 25 min. **TOTAL:** 1 hour 5 min.

- 1 **lb. lean ground beef**
- 1 **large onion, chopped**
- 2 **cups TACO BELL® HOME ORIGINALS® Thick 'N Chunky Salsa**
- 1 **can (15 oz.) black beans, drained, rinsed**
- ¼ **cup KRAFT Zesty Italian Dressing**
- 2 **Tbsp. TACO BELL® HOME ORIGINALS® Taco Seasoning Mix**
- 6 **flour tortillas (8 inch)**
- 1 **cup BREAKSTONE'S or KNUDSEN Sour Cream**
- 1 **pkg. (8 oz.) KRAFT Mexican Style Shredded Four Cheese**

HEAT oven to 400°F. Brown meat with onions in large skillet on medium-high heat; drain. Stir in salsa, beans, dressing and seasoning mix.

PLACE 3 tortillas in single layer on bottom of 13×9-inch baking dish; cover with layers of ½ each meat mixture, sour cream and cheese. Repeat layers. Cover with foil.

BAKE 30 min. Remove foil. Bake 10 min. or until casserole is heated through and cheese is melted. Let stand 5 min.

Makes 8 servings.

Make Ahead: Line 13×9-inch baking dish with foil, with ends of foil extending over sides of dish. Assemble recipe in prepared dish as directed. Cover with foil. Freeze up to 3 months. When ready to serve, heat oven to 400°F. Bake, covered, 1 hour. Remove foil. Bake an additional 15 to 20 min. or until casserole is heated through and cheese is melted. Let stand 5 min. before cutting to serve. To decrease the baking time, thaw casserole in refrigerator overnight, then bake, uncovered, 45 min. or until casserole is heated through and cheese is melted.

Serving Suggestion: Top with chopped tomatoes, shredded lettuce and cilantro just before serving.

Family Fun: Set out bowls of chopped lettuce, tomatoes and avocados so everyone can help themselves to their favorite toppings.

TACO BELL® and HOME ORIGINALS® are trademarks owned and licensed by Taco Bell Corp.

PASTA

Garden-Fresh Pasta Salad

PREP: 20 min. **TOTAL:** 1 hour 30 min. (incl. refrigerating)

- 1   **pkg. (1 lb.) farfalle (bow-tie pasta), uncooked**
- 2   **cups broccoli florets**
- 1   **small red onion, thinly sliced**
- 1   **red bell pepper, chopped**
- 1   **cup halved cherry tomatoes**
- 1   **bottle (8 oz.) KRAFT Sun-Dried Tomato Dressing**
- ½   **cup KRAFT Grated Parmesan Cheese**

COOK pasta as directed on package, adding broccoli for the last 3 min. Drain; rinse under cold water. Drain well; place in large bowl.

ADD onions, peppers and tomatoes; mix lightly. Toss with dressing.

REFRIGERATE 1 hour. Stir before serving; sprinkle with cheese.

Makes 14 servings, ¾ cup each.

Substitute: Substitute 1-inch asparagus pieces for the broccoli.

Substitute: Prepare using **KRAFT** Shredded Parmesan Cheese; or **KRAFT** Shredded Parmesan, Romano and Asiago Cheese.

Simply Lasagna

PREP: 20 min. **TOTAL:** 1 hour 20 min.

- 1 **lb. ground beef**
- 1 **egg, beaten**
- 2½ cups **KRAFT** Shredded Low-Moisture Part-Skim Mozzarella Cheese, divided
- 1 **container (15 oz.) POLLY-O Natural Part Skim Ricotta Cheese**
- ½ cup **KRAFT** Grated Parmesan Cheese, divided
- ¼ cup chopped fresh parsley
- 1 jar (26 oz.) spaghetti sauce
- 1 cup water
- 12 lasagna noodles, uncooked

HEAT oven to 350°F. Brown meat in large skillet. Meanwhile, mix egg, 1¼ cups mozzarella cheese, ricotta cheese, ¼ cup Parmesan cheese and parsley.

DRAIN meat; return to skillet. Stir in sauce. Add water to empty sauce jar; cover with lid and shake well. Stir into meat. Spread 1 cup sauce onto bottom of 13×9-inch baking dish; top with layers of 3 noodles, ⅓ ricotta cheese mixture and 1 cup sauce. Repeat layers twice. Top with remaining noodles, sauce and cheeses. Cover with greased foil.

BAKE 45 min. Remove foil; bake 15 min. or until heated through. Let stand 15 min.

Makes 12 servings.

Size-Wise: Since this comfort-food classic serves 12, it's a perfect dish to serve at your next gathering.

Easy Cleanup: Greasing the foil before using to cover the lasagna will help prevent the cheese from sticking to it.

Shortcut: Adding water to the sauce helps cook traditional noodles during baking, so you don't have to cook them beforehand. This saves you 15 to 20 min. of prep time.

Fettuccine Alfredo

PREP: 5 min. **TOTAL:** 20 min.

4 oz. (½ of 8-oz. pkg.) **PHILADELPHIA** Cream Cheese, cubed

½ cup **KRAFT** Grated Parmesan Cheese

¾ cup milk

¼ cup (½ stick) butter or margarine

¼ tsp. white pepper

⅛ tsp. garlic powder

8 oz. fettuccine, cooked, drained

⅛ tsp. ground nutmeg

PLACE cream cheese, Parmesan cheese, milk, butter, white pepper and garlic powder in medium saucepan; cook and stir on low heat until cream cheese is melted.

TOSS with hot fettuccine. Sprinkle with nutmeg.

Makes 4 servings, about 1 cup each.

Serving Suggestion: Try serving with Italian bread and a mixed green salad tossed with your favorite **KRAFT** Dressing, such as Balsamic Vinaigrette.

Special Extra: Prepare as directed, heating 1 pkg. (6 oz.) **OSCAR MAYER** Grilled or Italian Style Chicken Breast Strips with the sauce before tossing with pasta.

Substitute: Prepare using **PHILADELPHIA** Neufchâtel Cheese.

Low-Fat Zesty Shrimp and Pasta

PREP: 10 min. **TOTAL:** 25 min.

- ½ lb. linguine, uncooked
- ¾ cup prepared **GOOD SEASONS** Zesty Italian Salad Dressing & Recipe Mix for Fat Free Dressing, divided
- 2 cups sliced fresh mushrooms
- 1 small onion, thinly sliced
- 1 can (14 oz.) artichoke hearts, drained, quartered
- 1 lb. uncooked deveined peeled large shrimp
- 1 Tbsp. chopped fresh parsley
- ¼ cup **KRAFT** Grated Parmesan Cheese

COOK pasta in large saucepan as directed on package.

MEANWHILE, heat ½ cup dressing in large skillet on medium heat. Stir in mushrooms, onions and artichokes; cook and stir 3 min. or until onions are crisp-tender. Add shrimp and parsley; stir. Cook 2 min. or until shrimp turn pink, stirring occasionally.

DRAIN pasta; return to pan. Toss with shrimp mixture and remaining dressing; sprinkle with cheese.

Makes 6 servings.

Substitute: Prepare substituting scallops for the shrimp and 1 large red bell pepper, chopped, for the artichoke hearts.

Substitute: Prepare using **KRAFT** Light House Italian Dressing.

Better-than-Ever Cheesy Meat Lasagna

PREP: 30 min. **TOTAL:** 1 hour 10 min.

- ¾ lb. extra lean ground beef
- 3 cloves garlic, minced
- 1½ tsp. dried oregano leaves
- 1 jar (26 oz.) spaghetti sauce
- 1 large tomato, chopped
- 1 egg, beaten
- 1 container (16 oz.) **BREAKSTONE'S** or **KNUDSEN** Low Fat Cottage Cheese
- ¼ cup **KRAFT** Grated Parmesan Cheese
- 9 lasagna noodles, cooked, drained
- 2 cups **KRAFT** 2% Milk Shredded Mozzarella Cheese, divided

HEAT oven to 375°F. Brown meat with garlic and oregano in medium saucepan. Stir in spaghetti sauce; simmer 5 min., stirring occasionally. Remove from heat; stir in tomatoes.

MIX egg, cottage cheese and Parmesan cheese; spread ½ cup onto bottom of 13×9-inch baking dish. Top with layers of 3 noodles, 1 cup cottage cheese mixture, ½ cup mozzarella cheese and 1 cup of the remaining spaghetti sauce mixture. Repeat layers. Top with remaining noodles and spaghetti sauce mixture. Cover with foil.

BAKE 30 min. or until heated through. Top with remaining cheese. Bake, uncovered, 5 min. or until cheese is melted. Let stand 5 min.

Makes 9 servings.

Make Ahead: Assemble lasagna as directed; cover. Refrigerate up to 24 hours. When ready to serve, bake, covered, at 375°F for 40 min. or until heated through.

Cheesy Stuffed Shells

PREP: 30 min. **TOTAL:** 57 min.

- 1 jar (26 oz.) spaghetti sauce
- 1 large tomato, chopped
- 1 container (16 oz.) **BREAKSTONE'S** or **KNUDSEN** Low Fat Cottage Cheese
- 1 pkg. (10 oz.) frozen chopped spinach, thawed, well drained
- 1 cup **KRAFT** 2% Milk Shredded Mozzarella Cheese, divided
- ¼ cup **KRAFT** Grated Parmesan Cheese
- 1 tsp. Italian seasoning
- 20 jumbo pasta shells, cooked, drained

HEAT oven to 400°F. Mix sauce and tomatoes; spoon ½ into 13×9-inch baking dish.

MIX cottage cheese, spinach, ½ cup mozzarella cheese, Parmesan cheese and seasoning; spoon into shells. Place in dish; top with remaining sauce mixture. Cover with foil.

BAKE 25 min. or until heated through. Top with remaining cheese. Bake, uncovered, 2 min. or until cheese is melted.

Makes 5 servings, 4 stuffed shells each.

Make it Easy: To help prevent the cheese from sticking to the foil, spray it with cooking spray before using to cover the unbaked shells.

Make Ahead: Assemble recipe as directed; cover. Refrigerate up to 24 hours. When ready to serve, bake, covered, at 400°F for 35 min. or until heated through. Top with remaining cheese; continue as directed.

Easy Chicken & Broccoli Alfredo

PREP: 10 min. **TOTAL:** 22 min.

- ½ **lb. fettuccine or spaghetti, uncooked**
- 2 **cups fresh broccoli florets**
- ¼ **cup KRAFT Zesty Italian Dressing**
- 1 **lb. boneless, skinless chicken breasts, cut into bite-size pieces**
- 1⅔ **cups milk**
- 4 **oz. (½ of 8-oz. pkg.) PHILADELPHIA Cream Cheese, cubed**
- ¼ **cup KRAFT Grated Parmesan Cheese**
- ½ **tsp. dried basil leaves**

COOK pasta as directed on package, adding broccoli for the last 2 min.

MEANWHILE, heat dressing in large nonstick skillet on medium-high heat. Add chicken; cook and stir 5 min. or until cooked through. Stir in milk, cream cheese, Parmesan cheese and basil. Bring to boil, stirring constantly. Cook 2 min. or until heated through.

DRAIN pasta mixture; return to pan. Add chicken mixture; mix lightly.

Makes 4 servings, 2 cups each.

Substitute: Substitute frozen peas, chopped red bell peppers or any of your favorite vegetables for the broccoli.

Creamy Pasta Primavera

PREP: 15 min. **TOTAL:** 30 min.

- 3 **cups penne pasta, uncooked**
- 2 **Tbsp. KRAFT Light Zesty Italian Dressing**
- 1½ **lb. boneless, skinless chicken breasts, cut into bite-size pieces**
- 2 **zucchini, cut into chunks**
- 1½ **cups cut-up fresh asparagus (1 inch lengths)**
- 1 **red bell pepper, chopped**
- 1 **cup fat-free reduced-sodium chicken broth**
- 4 **oz. (½ of 8-oz. pkg.) PHILADELPHIA Neufchâtel Cheese, cubed**
- ¼ **cup KRAFT Grated Parmesan Cheese**

COOK pasta in large saucepan as directed on package.

MEANWHILE, heat dressing in large skillet on medium heat. Add chicken and vegetables; cook 10 to 12 min. or until chicken is cooked through, stirring frequently. Add broth and Neufchâtel cheese; cook 1 min. or until cheese is melted, stirring constantly. Stir in Parmesan cheese.

DRAIN pasta; return to pan. Add chicken and vegetable mixture; toss lightly. Cook 1 min. or until heated through. (Sauce will thicken upon standing.)

Makes 6 servings, 1⅓ cups each.

Special Extra: Sprinkle with 2 Tbsp. chopped fresh chives or basil.

Substitute: Prepare using whatever vegetables you have on hand.

Spinach Lasagna

PREP: 25 min. **TOTAL:** 1 hour 10 min.

- 1 container (16 oz.) **BREAKSTONE'S** or **KNUDSEN** Low Fat Cottage Cheese
- 1 pkg. (10 oz.) frozen chopped spinach, thawed, well drained
- 3 cups **KRAFT** 2% Milk Shredded Mozzarella Cheese, divided
- ½ cup **KRAFT** Grated Parmesan Cheese, divided
- 2 eggs, beaten
- 1 jar (26 oz.) spaghetti sauce, divided
- 9 lasagna noodles, cooked, drained

HEAT oven to 350°F. Mix cottage cheese, spinach, 2 cups mozzarella cheese, ¼ cup Parmesan cheese and eggs.

LAYER 1 cup sauce, 3 noodles and ½ the cottage cheese mixture in 13×9-inch baking dish. Repeat layers. Top with remaining noodles, sauce and cheeses.

BAKE 45 min. or until heated through. Let stand 10 min. before serving.

Makes 9 servings.

Serving Suggestion: Serve with your favorite vegetable, such as sautéed zucchini and yellow squash.

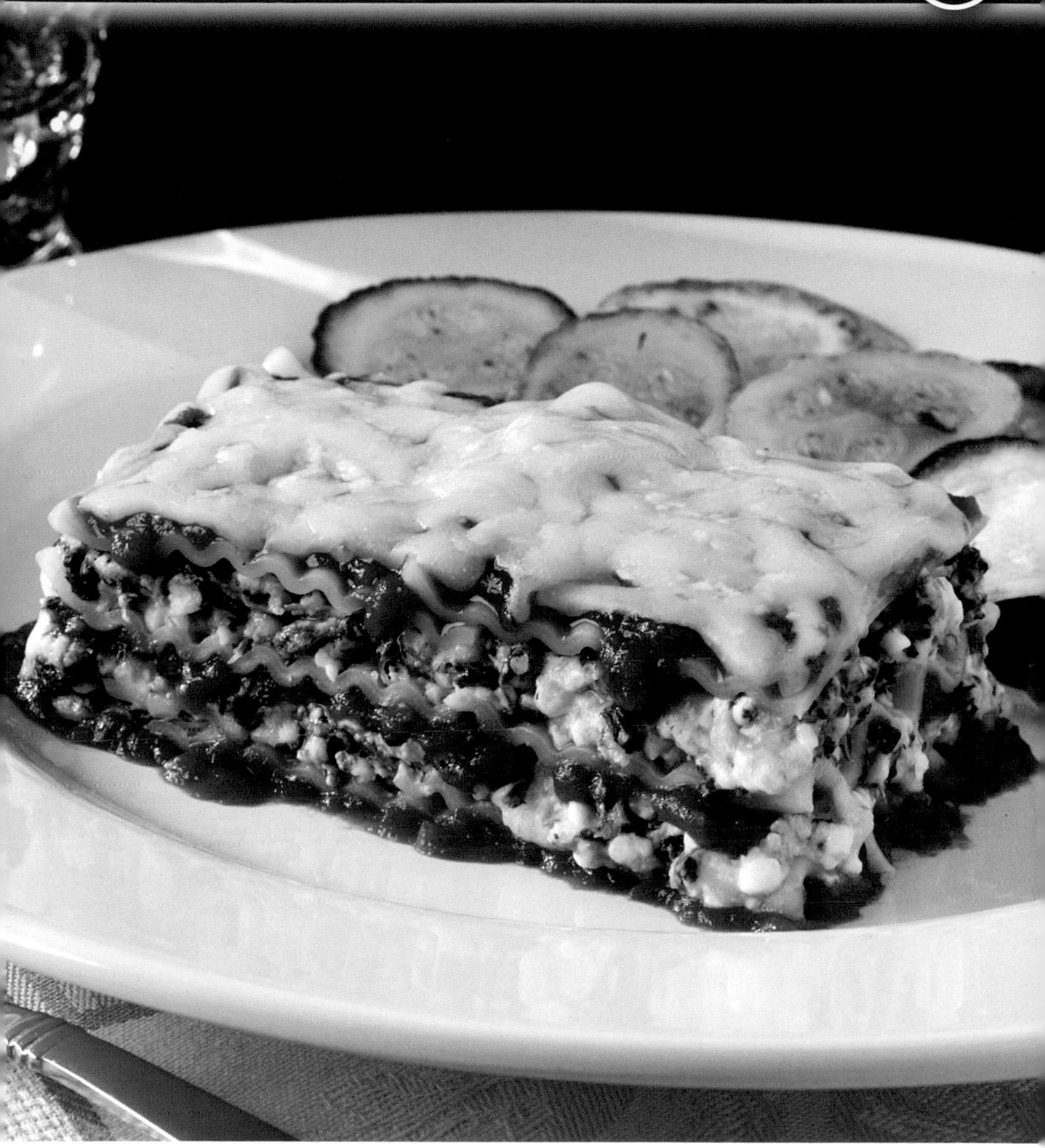

ENTRÉES

Easy Baked Parmesan Meatballs

PREP: 15 min. **TOTAL:** 40 min.

- 1 lb. ground beef
- ½ cup **KRAFT** Grated Parmesan Cheese
- ¼ cup chopped fresh parsley
- 1 egg, beaten
- 1 clove garlic, minced

HEAT oven to 375°F. Mix ingredients; shape into 12 meatballs.

PLACE in foil-lined 15×10×1-inch baking pan.

BAKE 25 min. or until cooked through.

Makes 6 servings, 2 meatballs each.

Serving Suggestion: Try serving with your favorite hot cooked pasta and sauce and a quick bagged salad tossed with your favorite **KRAFT** Dressing, such as House Italian.

Substitute: Substitute 1 Tbsp. parsley flakes for the chopped fresh parsley.

Chicken and Spinach Risotto

PREP: 10 min. **TOTAL:** 30 min.

   1 **lb. boneless, skinless chicken breasts, cut into bite-size pieces**
   1 **Tbsp. oil**
   4 **cups baby spinach leaves, cleaned**
1½ **cups instant white rice, uncooked**
   1 **cup grape or cherry tomatoes**
   1 **can (10½ oz.) condensed chicken broth**
   ½ **cup water**
   ¼ **cup KRAFT Grated Parmesan Cheese**

COOK chicken in hot oil in large deep nonstick skillet on medium heat 10 min. or until cooked through, stirring frequently.

ADD spinach, rice, tomatoes, broth and water; mix well. Bring to boil. Reduce heat to low; cover. Simmer 5 min., stirring occasionally.

STIR in cheese.

Makes 4 servings.

Substitute: Substitute dry white wine for ½ cup broth. Cover and refrigerate remaining broth for another use.

Substitute: Prepare using **KRAFT** Grated Three Cheese Blend.

Chicken-Parmesan Bundles

PREP: 35 min. **TOTAL:** 1 hour 5 min.

4 oz. (½ of 8-oz. pkg.) **PHILADELPHIA** Cream Cheese, softened

1 pkg. (10 oz.) frozen chopped spinach, thawed, well drained

1¼ cups **KRAFT** Shredded Low-Moisture Part-Skim Mozzarella Cheese, divided

6 Tbsp. **KRAFT** Grated Parmesan Cheese, divided

6 small boneless, skinless chicken breast halves (1½ lb.), pounded to ¼-inch thickness

1 egg

10 **RITZ** Crackers, crushed

1½ cups spaghetti sauce, heated

HEAT oven to 375°F. Mix cream cheese, spinach, 1 cup mozzarella cheese and 3 Tbsp. Parmesan cheese; spread onto chicken. Roll up tightly, starting at short ends. Secure with toothpicks, if desired.

BEAT egg in pie plate. Mix remaining Parmesan cheese and cracker crumbs in separate pie plate. Dip chicken in egg then in crumb mixture, turning to evenly coat both sides of each breast. Place, seam-sides down, in 13×9-inch baking dish sprayed with cooking spray.

BAKE 30 min. or until chicken is cooked through (165°F). Remove and discard toothpicks, if using. Top with spaghetti sauce and remaining mozzarella cheese.

Makes 6 servings.

Make Ahead: Assemble chicken bundles and place in baking dish as directed; refrigerate up to 4 hours. When ready to serve, bake at 375°F for 35 min. or until chicken is cooked through (165°F).

Special Extra: Stir chopped fresh basil and/or sliced black olives into spaghetti sauce before heating.

Foil-Wrapped Fish with Creamy Parmesan Sauce

PREP: 10 min. **TOTAL:** 22 min.

- **4** orange roughy fillets (1 lb.), thawed if frozen
- **¼** cup **KRAFT** Mayonnaise
- **¼** cup **KRAFT** Grated Parmesan Cheese
- **⅛** tsp. ground red pepper (cayenne)
- **2** zucchini, sliced
- **½** of a red bell pepper, cut into strips

HEAT grill to medium-high. Spray 4 (18×12-inch) sheets of heavy-duty foil with cooking spray; place 1 fillet in center of each. Spread with mayo; top with cheese, ground pepper and vegetables.

BRING up foil sides. Double fold top and ends to seal each packet, leaving room for heat circulation inside. Place on grill rack; cover grill with lid.

GRILL 10 to 12 min. or until fish flakes easily with fork.

Makes 4 servings.

Special Extra: Garnish each serving with lemon wedges.

Use Your Oven: Heat oven to 450°F. Assemble foil packets as directed; place on baking sheet. Bake 18 to 22 min. or until fish flakes easily with fork.

Parmesan Baked Salmon

PREP: 10 min. **TOTAL:** 25 min.

- ¼ cup **KRAFT** Mayonnaise
- 2 Tbsp. **KRAFT** Grated Parmesan Cheese
- ⅛ tsp. ground red pepper (cayenne)
- 4 salmon fillets (1 lb.), skin removed
- 2 tsp. lemon juice
- 10 **RITZ** Crackers, crushed

HEAT oven to 400°F. Mix mayo, cheese and pepper.

PLACE fish in foil-lined baking pan; top with lemon juice, mayo mixture and crumbs.

BAKE 12 to 15 min. or until fish flakes easily with fork.

Makes 4 servings.

Special Extra: Add ¼ tsp. dill weed to the mayo mixture before spreading onto fish.

Serving Suggestion: Serve with your favorite green vegetables, such as fresh green beans.

Easy Parmesan-Garlic Chicken

PREP: 5 min. **TOTAL:** 30 min.

- ½ cup **KRAFT** Grated Parmesan Cheese
- 1 env. **GOOD SEASONS** Italian Salad Dressing & Recipe Mix
- ½ tsp. garlic powder
- 6 boneless, skinless chicken breast halves (2 lb.)

HEAT oven to 400°F. Mix cheese, dressing mix and garlic powder.

MOISTEN chicken with water; coat with cheese mixture. Place in single layer in shallow baking dish.

BAKE 20 to 25 min. or until chicken is cooked through (165°F).

Makes 6 servings, 1 chicken breast each.

Special Extra: For a golden appearance after chicken is cooked through, set oven to Broil. Place 6 inches from heat source. Broil 2 to 4 min. or until chicken is golden brown.

Serving Suggestion: Serve with mixed green salad, tossed with your favorite **KRAFT** Dressing.

Parmesan-Crusted Chicken in Cream Sauce

PREP: 15 min. **TOTAL:** 30 min.

2 cups instant brown rice, uncooked

1 can (14 oz.) fat-free reduced-sodium chicken broth, divided

6 **RITZ** Crackers, finely crushed

2 Tbsp. **KRAFT** Grated Parmesan Cheese

4 small boneless, skinless chicken breast halves (1 lb.)

2 tsp. oil

⅓ cup **PHILADELPHIA** Chive & Onion Light Cream Cheese Spread

¾ lb. asparagus spears, trimmed, steamed

COOK rice as directed on package, using 1¼ cups broth and ½ cup water. Meanwhile, mix cracker crumbs and Parmesan cheese on plate. Moisten chicken with water, shaking off excess; coat both sides with crumb mixture. (Discard any remaining crumb mixture.)

HEAT oil in large nonstick skillet on medium heat. Add chicken; cook 5 to 6 min. on each side or until golden brown and cooked through (165°F). Place on serving plate; cover to keep warm.

ADD remaining broth and cream cheese spread to skillet. Bring just to boil, stirring constantly; simmer 3 min. or until thickened, stirring frequently. Spoon over chicken. Serve with rice and asparagus.

Makes 4 servings.

Variation: Prepare using **PHILADELPHIA** Light Cream Cheese Spread and stirring in 1 Tbsp. chopped fresh chives with the cream cheese spread.

Storing Asparagus: To store asparagus, stand fresh spears upright in a container filled with about 1 inch of water. Cover loosely with a plastic bag and refrigerate. Or, store in refrigerator with a damp paper towel wrapped around base of stalks and cover loosely with a plastic bag. Asparagus is best when cooked the day it is purchased, but will keep up to 3 or 4 days. Wash just before using.

Cheese & Chicken Fajita Quesadillas

PREP: 15 min. **TOTAL:** 32 min.

½ **lb. boneless, skinless chicken breasts, cut into thin strips**

¾ **cup each: sliced onions and red pepper strips**

½ **cup salsa**

½ **cup drained canned black beans, rinsed**

6 **flour tortillas (6 inch)**

1½ **cups KRAFT 2% Milk Shredded Sharp Cheddar Cheese**

Cook chicken in large skillet sprayed with cooking spray on medium-high heat 5 min., stirring frequently.

Add onions and peppers; cook 4 to 5 min. or until crisp-tender. Stir in salsa and beans; cook 3 min. or until heated through, stirring occasionally.

Top tortillas with chicken mixture and cheese; fold in half. Spray second large skillet with cooking spray. Heat on medium heat. Add quesadillas, in batches; cook 2 min. on each side or until evenly browned. Cut in half to serve.

Makes 6 servings, 1 quesadilla each.

Variation: Prepare as directed, substituting ½ cup drained canned corn for the black beans. Serve topped with shredded romaine lettuce, chopped fresh tomatoes and chopped cilantro.

Special Extra: Top each serving with 1 Tbsp. **BREAKSTONE'S** Reduced Fat or **KNUDSEN** Light Sour Cream.

Note: If you have only 1 large skillet, cook chicken mixture in skillet as directed, then transfer to bowl; cover to keep warm. Wipe out skillet, then spray with additional cooking spray and use to cook quesadillas as directed.

Eggplant Parmesan

PREP: 10 min. **TOTAL:** 50 min.

  1 **eggplant (1 lb.), sliced**

  ½ **lb. sliced fresh mushrooms**

  ½ **cup KRAFT Grated Parmesan Cheese, divided**

1½ **cups KRAFT 2% Milk Shredded Mozzarella Cheese, divided**

  1 **jar (26 oz.) spaghetti sauce**

HEAT oven to 400°F. Place ½ each of the eggplant and mushrooms in 13×9-inch baking pan sprayed with cooking spray; top with ⅓ of each cheese. Repeat layers.

TOP with sauce; cover with foil.

BAKE 35 min. Sprinkle with remaining cheeses. Bake, uncovered, 5 min. or until mozzarella cheese is melted.

Makes 6 servings.

Serving Suggestion: Serve with a mixed green salad, tossed with your favorite **KRAFT** Dressing.

Special Extra: Garnish with fresh basil for an extra burst of flavor.

CHICKEN

CHOCOLATE

DIPS & SPREADS

FISH & SEAFOOD

SIDES & SNACKS